STAGES OF CONSCIOUSNESS

STAGES OF CONSCIOUSNESS

*Meditations on The Boundaries
of the Soul*

GEORG   KÜHLEWIND

TRANSLATED BY MARIA ST. GOAR

EDITED BY CHRISTOPHER BAMFORD
AND FRED PADDOCK

INNER TRADITIONS LINDISFARNE PRESS

This book is a translation of *Bewusstseinsstufen, Meditationen über die Grenzen der Seele* by Georg Kühlewind, published by Verlag Freies Geistesleben. © 1976 Verlag Freies Geistesleben GmbH, Stuttgart.

Chapters Four, Five, and Eight appeared as independent essays in *Die Drei*, vols. 42 and 43, Stuttgart 1972 and 1973.

This edition © 1984 The Lindisfarne Press

AN INNER TRADITIONS / LINDISFARNE PRESS BOOK

Published by The Lindisfarne Press
Box 127, West Stockbridge, MA 01266 U.S.A.

Distributed to the book trade
by Inner Traditions International.
All inquiries should be addressed to
377 Park Avenue South, New York, NY 10016
U.S.A.
ISBN 0-89281-065-3

Printed in the United States of America

CONTENTS

ACKNOWLEDGEMENTS

The editors and publisher would like to thank the following for their help in the production of this book: Caryl Johnston, Michael Lipson, John Miller, Mado Spiegler, Elfin Vogel.

The publisher would also like to acknowledge with gratitude the financial assistance it has received for the publication of this book from the Cultural Freedom Fund of the Tides Foundation, as well as from many kind people, some of whom not only sent in advance subscriptions but also made generous contributions to a fund for the publication of works by Georg Kühlewind.

INTRODUCTION

BY CHRISTOPHER BAMFORD

THE critical situation that human beings face today as a consequence of the dominance of abstract, calculative thinking may be traced to the fundamental rift that places the human subject "inside," over against a world that is "outside." By this ancient wound the world has been desecrated. Despoiled of all but utilitarian significance, extinction faces it. The situation is dramatic. The feeling is that "only a god can save us now." But who still believes in gods? We feel that we come too late for the gods or that we have killed them. We feel ourselves to be alone — and yet not alone. Discovering the need to rely upon ourselves, to found the world anew, we sense a god within, who, since God is dead, suggests a new order of participation in reality. "Ineffable is the union of man and God in every act of the soul," wrote Emerson, who also knew: "We first share the life by which things exist and afterwards see them as appearances in nature and forget that we have shared their cause."[1] On the discovery and realization of this reality — Emerson calls it "the fountain of action and the fountain of thought" — depends more than we can say.

More bluntly stated: since egoism is the arrogation of all meaning and value to oneself, we may say that everything hangs on the ability of human beings to overcome their egoism and meet the world in its true being. This egoism is but nihilism by another name. Egoism/nihilism has stripped the world of its qualities and rendered it meaningless. It has quite simply killed it. And thereby human life too has become meaningless and dead. For if human life is not a part of the world, of what is it a part? Pursuing the unreality and meaninglessness of the sensory world, human beings have become unreal and meaningless to themselves also. Behind this lies the original superstition of an autonomous, self-constituted world of thought, able by its own self-verifying logic to mirror and map a vast, unthinking, objective universe. All of this — that the universe is vast (in this sense), unthinking and objective — is nonsense. Nor are we who we think we are. Yet, in order to maintain itself, this superstition — which has a philosophical name, but which we may simply term "egoism" — constantly shores up its illusions by maintaining that, according to its own logic, all alternatives are, if not false, then as unfalsifiable as dreams. But we forget that we ourselves are "such stuff as dreams are made on." In other words, associated with the rift between inside and outside is another abyss between what is "rational," i.e., conscious, and what is "irrational," i.e., preconscious. We take each of these as fixed and never consider that what is preconscious may derive either from "below" or from "above" — i.e., be either "subconscious" or "superconscious." At the same time, we fail to notice that consciousness itself is always a process and never a product.

To overcome this situation of pervasive doubt, paranoia and unreality, some self-existent ground must be found out of which the sacramental values of truth, beauty and goodness may be renewed and embodied in human experience. Rudolf Steiner dedicated his life to this task: to showing that human self-knowledge may pass beyond limited egoical self-consciousness and self-feeling into the realm of the real. "The destiny of the self is that only in its separation from the universe can it find contact with the universe. Man would not be man if as an I he were not separated from everything else; but he would not be man in the highest sense if, as such a separated I, he did not enlarge himself out of himself to the All-I. Above all, it is characteristic of human nature that it should overcome a contradiction which originally lies within it."[2] Within this paradoxical movement of reversal—from "little I" to "big I"—lies contemporary humanity's means of self-transcendence, i.e., the means whereby human beings today may penetrate ever more deeply and consciously into the creative foundation of things in order to reveal (and redeem) there the heart and divine-human self-identity of all that is. This is what it means to become a "son of God." True self-knowledge reveals the real self as participating in, and participated by, the creative knowledge—the love underlying life, matter, consciousness, etc.—who is the originary being of the universe: the I AM or (solar) Logos. It is to this Pauline and Anthroposophical (Steiner) tradition—"Not I, but the Christ in me"—that Georg Kühlewind belongs.

This tradition is distinguished by the fact that it begins with thinking and modern self-consciousness—thinking, by which we receive everything and are everything but of which we know nothing, precisely because we are modern, Cartesian-Kantian self-conscious beings. Everything that we are and know, every perception and self-perception that enters our consciousness, derives from thinking and is expressed for us in thoughts which, as Cartesian-Kantian isolated subjects, we take to be the only reality accessible to us. Hence we live under the tyranny of habit, captives of the past. Yet thoughts, by which we know that we have thought without ever knowing that we are thinking, constitute not only a prison for us but also the intimation of escape from it. For thoughts are the deadened residue, the crystallization, of something that was once alive and dynamic — a living process that reaches us in arrested concepts and ideas, which we then passively allow by force of habit to usurp the living reality of the world. These ideas and pictures become the apparently fixed and insurmountable boundaries between ourselves and the world, and the I-It relationship takes hold. Immured within our representations, hypnotized by them, we begin to worship them as idols. Yet what was alive, and is living still, beyond the limited boundaries of our ego, unites us to the world. As immediacy or intuition, we sense it as the source of all our thoughts and perceptions. The I-Thou relationship is primordial. In our heart of hearts we know that the world medium within which we live and move and have our being is a thinking or cognizing one. As Kühlewind says, taking the exception, the inversion, to prove the rule, even the fact that the world seems outside and opposed is a purely mental construct. Everything in the world bears the signature of thinking — but thinking as life and love — and is, as we receive it, a residue of that thinking deadened by our habitual doubt, our dualized, dialectical, comparing consciousness. We are the world, always. Our tired, suffering, hungry lives — our alienation, apathy, hopelessness — are its too. There is only one world. Beyond, behind, before the finished perceptions and thoughts that rudely slice our experience of the world into two lies a single reality—the true universe—and we are it. Thinking and perceiving, in fact and in principle, are direct and unmediated. The mediation and separation that we experience is only a by-product of human individuation and can be overcome. There is a single reality to which we belong; thinking and perceiving are but approaches to it. There are not two worlds—inside and outside, subjective and objective, thought and seen, spiritual and material—but only one world, "spiritual" in essence, "cognizing" in nature. The inside of the world is the inside of humanity. Full reality is the magical interpenetration and cooperation of the one in the other, without mediation, without arrestation. "In truth, the sense world is also a spiritual world."[3]

Because we depend on it, we know nothing about thinking. It is the only process that we cannot learn more about by thinking about it. To think about thinking only delays the issue, restricting it to an indefinite regression at the level of what has been thought. To uncover the inner nature and secret gift of thinking a new faculty of experience must be developed—a deeper phenomenology or level of consciousness by the means of which we may observe thinking *non-dualistically*, that is, not observe but *live* it, think it in the present: to become ourselves the presence of thinking.

To reach this awareness, Kühlewind begins with the distinction between thoughts and thinking. All that we usually call thinking is thought: the juxtaposition and association of finished, past—hence dead—thoughts. These thoughts must have been living once—indeed, every new moment of understanding is a breath from the level of what is living and present — but all our conscious experience is limited to the remnants, to what has dropped from presence into the rigid framework of the psychological time of mutually exclusive passing moments, whose present moment inevitably escapes us. Our consciousness is of this past alone, of what we have already thought (we cannot recall when). The first realization, therefore, is that what we call thinking is only a kind of exteriorization or mechanical rearrangement of fragments of another, more vital process, and that behind our passive, petrified thoughts must lie an active world of living thinking, of which we know nothing, precisely because it is concealed from us by our thoughts. We are imprisoned by our thoughts, yet our thoughts — and the space, the gaps, between them — must continually indicate the way out of the prison. Where do thoughts come from? Who or what is their source?

In this tradition, then, the task is to experience the active nature of thinking: to bring thinking, which is activity — continuous presence — into conscious experience, which in a sense is also continuous presence. For the more fully we experience something, the more we discover that we have overcome the dead weight of "pastness" (egoism) and begin to live in the present, in presence. Ordinarily, with reference to thinking, we call this peak experience "intuition." Steiner and Kühlewind propose a way or method of inner schooling in that state of consciousness which we occasionally glimpse as intuition. They would have us live that state, or at least begin to do so.

To begin to live in intuition is to begin to leave the ego's conditioned, relative world of attachments, desires and fears, for the real world of self-sustaining spiritual essences or realities. "When we live in thinking we live in the self-supporting spiritual web of being."[4] We experience a state no longer conditioned by the organism, i.e., it is brain-free. To live in intuition is to leave the soul's artifactual, illusionist world, which in terms of its individuated consciousness is the seed-shadow or premonition of its real individuation or spiritualization, for the monistic world of the spirit. Thinking at this stage ceases to be ratiocination and becomes "an experience — in pure spirit — of a purely spiritual content."[5] This has to do with becoming inwardly present in an identity. Inner and outer are united in a higher nature, a higher cognizing activity that unites feeling and willing in a single deed of *love*. It is as if "organ" and "object" of perception become one in the act of cognition itself, and the subject becomes the presence of this act, present to it. Just so, the ancient alchemists spoke of being present at the creation. No wonder, for in this act we encounter the universal cognitive-ontological presence, the I AM. Indeed, just as our thoughts construct the artifactual ego, living thinking which is their womb is the being and beginning of the true self and true being. The human being who is called to know himself must endure the ego's death in order to raise his consciousness to the life of the spirit and meet himself there. It is the ego's death itself which is the light of the true self's birth. The ego, the soul, even in its highest manifestation, cannot experience spirit. Only spirit can experience spirit. Therefore the soul must become spirit, one with its spirit. Hence the soul's only task, once it has found itself, is to lose itself: to lay itself down in surrender. In the soul's surrender, spirit appears. But in order to surrender, soul must have something

to surrender. Hence the profound need of separation, individuation. It was for this reason, perhaps, that Christ said
that He came to save sinners.

Thinking is unique in that, like light, it is transparent. It
is at once process and product. We cannot think it. We depend upon it, but we are unaware of it. It is our element,
interpenetrating all we do and are. Therefore it seems
closest to us, to who we are. Yet we cannot separate ourselves from it. I know that I walk, I can separate myself
from my walking, but in the case of thinking it is different,
more difficult. Who can tell the dancer from the dance?
Yet there must be a thinker. Who thinks? Who am I? All
spiritual paths return to and hinge upon this riddle. As the
eye and the light of which it is an extension cannot see
themselves but are seeing, the I, which seems to be related
to thinking, seems unable to think itself. I am not body,
not soul—not any "thing"—*I am I.* That I, which is not
thinking but the thinker, is then closest to thinking, but
too involved with it. Connected to the task of the soul's
surrender, therefore, is that other task of the separation of
the subject from thinking.

To achieve this, thinking must be strengthened by the
practice of *attention*. First, attention to a theme, then attention without an object—pure attention or, as Kühlewind writes, "power, possibility, preparedness." It is
attention without an object, which is an exclusively psychic "energy" that brings us into the presence of pure activity. Now the I AM is. We become one with pure spiritual
activity. This is freedom, as God is free. Thus, according
to Jewish tradition, "This is the meaning of the verse 'I am
that I am'—I am named according to my acts."[6] Just so
too, in spiritual, brain-free cognition, activity is all.

Steiner writes: "The soul is only conscious of possessing a particular organ of spirit to the extent that it is able to make use of it. For these organs are not something static; they are in continual movement. And when they are not employed, it is not possible to be conscious of their presence. Thus, their apprehension and their use coincide."[7]

By the purely psychic practice of attention, the true subject, no longer identified with thinking, is revealed as pure activity, pure relatedness, invisible, indemonstrable, a nothing. But a nothing which is everything. Of this true self, Kühlewind writes, we can only say that it is. Resting on nothing, it draws its meaning, which is activity, at once out of itself and in identity with meaning, the primal activity. It is a god, a personal-impersonal cosmic being. And, because it is, it can lay itself down with complete altruism: it can merge without fear of loss of self in being. It has nothing to lose. Hence the possibility of true cognitive love arises, of which the artifactual ego's surrender was but a weak premonition.

Therefore this path of thinking, like all spiritual paths, is a path of surrender—an activity, a way, a praxis. To be able to walk this path is to realize in the most fundamental way possible the human promise of freedom. It is to engage in the unmediated reading of the world—a reading which is a listening and a playing. By this, the world continually unveils itself to itself through us. We are it and its transformation.

Because of this, something should be said of Kühlewind's logic, which is not the closed, linear logic of ordinary philosophical thought and description, but an open, evocative logic of seeking-and-finding—the free, hermeneutical logic of a path laid down in seeking. Logic, of course, derives from *logos*, which means not only "word" but also, and more generally, *ratio* or relationship. It is not therefore something fixed and rigid but refers rather to a living network of connections (ratios) that, binding together and holding apart, create a coherent whole or identity. From this point of view, Kühlewind's logic is above all a logic of experience. In order for its truth to be realized, it must be lived. Testifying to his own experience, Kühlewind seeks to evoke it in another. Calling his readers to experience what he has experienced, he enjoins them to do as he has done. In this sense his writing is closer to the injunctive mode of a musical score or a mathematical text than it is to normal, informational-descriptive discourse. Kühlewind, in fact, gives us very little "objective information," and a reader seeking simply to be informed will come away disappointed. *Stages of Consciousness* demands an active, participatory reading. Kühlewind starts out his essays by casting a wide net and loosely marshalling the different concepts he will need. Thereby he unfolds a field of "idea-phenomena" which, as we examine them more closely, seem to spring from and lead towards a single, powerfully formative conception. As the essays progress, their reasoning becomes increasingly focussed and the reader's attention is drawn towards a paradigmatic or archetypal moment, of which, it now becomes clear, the opening ideas and concepts were just modes.

Stages of Consciousness, then, is a book of philosophy which goes beyond philosophy in that in it philosophy moves to another level and becomes *experience*. It bears witness. Western philosophy itself, as Heidegger has clearly shown, leads inexorably to this moment, this need. Here philosophy, having died, is born again.

NOTES

1. Ralph Waldo Emerson, "The Over-Soul," "Self-Reliance,"
   Essays (New York: Thomas Crowell, 1961).
2. Rudolf Steiner, *Eleven European Mystics* (Blauvelt, N.Y.:
   Rudolf Steiner Publications, 1971).
3. Rudolf Steiner, *The Philosophy of Freedom* (Spring Valley,
   N.Y.: Anthroposophical Press, 1964).
4. *Ibid.*
5. *Ibid.*
6. Ephraim E. Urbach, *The Sages*, (Jerusalem: The Magnes
   Press, The Hebrew University, 1979).
7. Rudolf Steiner, *The Case for Anthroposophy* (London: Rudolf Steiner Press, 1970).

Since writing *Stages of Consciousness*—his first book—in the years 1972–1974, Georg Kühlewind has published the following books in German:

1978   *Die Wahrheit Tun, Erfahrungen und Konsequenzen des intuitiven Denkens*
       (*Doing the Truth, Experiences and Consequences of Intuitive Thinking*)

1979   *Das Gewahrwerden des Logos, Die Wissenschaft des Evangelisten Johannes*
       (*Becoming Aware of the Logos, The Knowledge of John the Evangelist*)

1981   *Die Diener des Logos, Der Mensch als Wort und Gespräch*
       (*Servants of the Logos, the Human Being as Word and Conversation*)

1982   *Das Leben der Seele zwischen Überbewusstsein und Unterbewusstsein, Elemente einer spirituellen Psychologie*
       (*The Life of the Soul between Supraconsciousness and Subconsciousness, Elements of a Spiritual Psychology*)

1983   *Von Normalen zum Gesunden, Wege zur Befreiung des erkrankten Bewusstseins*
       (*From Normality to Health, Ways of Freeing the Sick Consciousness*)

1984   *Das Licht des Wortes: Welt, Sprache, Meditation*
       (*The Light of the Word: World, Language, Meditation*)

FOREWORD

Modern humanity's most difficult task is to become aware of, to see and to overcome the threshold of mirrored consciousness. The first essay attempts to show how Rudolf Steiner proposes reaching this goal in his *Philosophy of Freedom*. Consideration of the threshold lying between thinking and what has been thought leads the one making this experiment to "the fundamental experience of the spirit." The third essay attempts to develop a methodology for the first steps in the realm of concentration and contemplation. The last essays set forth the outcome: how, in the observation of the soul's boundaries, these boundaries become transparent and permeable. The form of the communication is such that the reader, tracing the lines of the movements of thinking, steps into its fabric.

The Two Stages of
Consciousness

THE BOUNDARIES OF THINKING

IT IS relatively easy for a human being today to bring the boundaries of his thinking and thereby also those of his consciousness into the realm of experience. This may even be done in a variety of ways. One need only ask, *Why* is something evident? What constitutes "evidence"? Why is the logical logical? Thinking knows no answer to these questions—or rather each attempt to answer has to presuppose what is being questioned. Hence the discomfort caused by such questions and the consequent avoidance of them, resulting involuntarily in promoting the decline of thinking consciousness to a precritical, naive level, that of the unreflecting use of thinking. Hence too the half-thought-through attempts to regulate or schematize thinking in order to make it "correct"—without ever recognizing that regulation itself occurs through thinking and must be understood and evaluated through thinking that itself is not yet "regulated." One is often unaware that logic derives *from* thinking, not the reverse. *First* one thinks logically, *then* one creates or comprehends logic as a descriptive, not a normative science. The latter always presupposes logical thinking.[1]

But the approach to the boundary can also take other

forms. Wittgenstein determined that "language" provides clear-cut forms of expression only for the simplest statements. (He really means not forms of language, but forms of thinking.) It is easily demonstrated, however, that the simplest statement — for instance, "Here is the table" — contains elements which actually can neither be seen through nor even thought through. In the sentence quoted, the word and concept "is" is obviously one which cannot be gotten to the bottom of, for who could explain its meaning? The child grasps this concept — like all others — intuitively and unconsciously, uses it without error, and continues to do so as an adult. The concept "here" is just as inexplicable. To elucidate it, at least the concept "there" is necessary. Each of these concepts is inexplicable in itself. To understand either one, the intuition "here-there" is necessary, and although this intuition can be approached, it cannot be summoned forth or "made understandable" through other concepts. The word and concept "table" seems the most accessible to us. But try to explain or define it: leaving aside the non-intrinsic characteristics (compositional material, number of legs, form, etc.), we are left with horizontal surface, hardness, limited size and height. It is easily demonstrated, however, that even these are not decisive. A beer keg can serve as a "table." It is considered fashionable at times to use the floor as a "table," and at a picnic a cloth laid on the slope of a hill can serve as a "table." So the "table" has had to relinquish all properties recognized as inherent to it. With this complete dematerialization and stripping of form, only the "function" remains — the "serving" aspect of the table. What does the function consist in? To serve for eating, writing, card playing, chess playing, etc., all of which can be neither defined nor indicated with conceptual exactness. Still, the intuition remains: everyone "knows" what a table is, after all, or what serves as a table under a given circumstance.

Going only a step further, we see that to establish the "meaning" of single words on a rational basis, without reference to the faculty of intuition, is simply impossible. This becomes very clear in the case of concepts that do not stem from the perceived world. For instance, the meaning of the socioeconomic word "work" is vigorously disputed and can be clarified only by calling on further concepts for help. Should one wish to pursue this process, perhaps by trying to find a basis in "convention," still more concepts must be utilized, and it becomes obvious that this effort to clarify ends in unmanageable divergence. Finally, it is our mutual trust that we all understand what *that* means that makes communication possible.

It is clear from these few examples that the paradoxical situation of having concepts that are easily used but, as regards their origin, basically unclear stems from the fact that consciousness only "experiences" the already-thought, whereas the *process* of thinking lies *before* what has been thought. Therefore this process—the coming into being of thought—is preconscious. Without finished thoughts and finished representations, there is no consciousness in the usual sense of the word. To "empty" one's consciousness is ordinarily impossible. Attempting to achieve it, we drift into a kind of dreaming or sleep.[2]

THINKING ABOUT THINKING

The first half of Rudolf Steiner's *The Philosophy of Freedom* deals with a stage of consciousness that may be characterized by the fact that, at this stage, the contents of consciousness are given through observation. In particular, this field of consciousness is most suited for the observation of thinking—or, more accurately, the already-thought. What is meant by "thinking" in the first seven chapters of *The Philosophy of Freedom* is not the process itself but, as in the ordinary usage of the word, the result of this process as it enters consciousness. This becomes particularly clear when Steiner speaks of the observation of thinking:

> I am, moreover, in the same position when I enter into the exceptional state and reflect on my own thinking. I can never observe my present thinking; I can only subsequently take my experience of my thinking process as the object of fresh thinking. If I wanted to watch my present thinking, I should have to split myself into two persons, one to think, the other to observe the thinking. But this I cannot do. I can only accomplish it in two separate acts. The thinking to be observed is never that in which I am actually engaged, but another one. . . .
>
> There are two things which are incompatible with one another: active production and its objective contemplation.

The intuitive character of the way in which thoughts arise is clarified in the following quotation:

> What a concept is cannot be expressed in words. Words can do no more than draw our attention to the fact that

we have concepts. . . .

In contrast to the content of the percept which is given to us from without, the content of thinking appears inwardly. The form in which this first makes its appearance we will call *intuition*. *Intuition* is for thinking what *observation* is for the percept.[3]

The "form," the way in which we "shape" concepts, is here called intuition. At first, however, we do not experience this "shaping," only the result of the intuition, because we are not capable of apprehending the presence of spirit in the shaping of concepts. We experience only the continual loss of presentness,[4] that is, what is always falling into pastness, the past, the finished concept. Try to grasp the present: Now! — it is already gone.

"When someone thinks, he really perceives only the last phases of his thinking activity, of his thinking experience."[5] Following this passage is a detailed description of the various phases of the thinking process. Examples of similar assertions related to perception are to be found in the first meditation of the booklet, *A Road to Self-Knowledge*.[6]

Before the age of the consciousness soul,* the possibility of observing finished thinking or of thinking about what has been thought did not exist. To be sure, the intellectual soul* makes the most incisive use of thinking,

---

*For a discussion of the consciousness soul and the intellectual soul, see Rudolf Steiner, *Theosophy*, Anthroposophical Press, New York, 1971, part one, section four, "Body, Soul and Spirit." And also Rudolf Steiner, *Anthroposophical Leading Thoughts*, Rudolf Steiner Press, London, 1973, pp. 69–131. Cf. Owen Barfield, *Romanticism Comes of Age*, Wesleyan University Press, Middletown, 1966, pp 84–103, 126–143. — Ed.

but this is always the *ancilla* of another principle — today, *ancilla technicae, ventris* ("servant of technology, of the stomach"), not to mention others — in any case, *ancilla corporis* ("servant of the body"). Thinking about thinking began during Scholasticism, which was a prelude to the consciousness soul. Descartes' dictum *Cogito ergo sum*, for all its inadequacies as a statement, is typical of the consciousness soul's attitude. Obviously, it is the capacity for pure, perception-free, abstract thinking that makes this reflection about thinking possible. But with this capacity, all the doubts about thinking, about cognizing, also arise: the age of epistemology arrives. Cognition is no longer accepted naively — it is thought about. Since this reflection is done with the same powers of cognition that are otherwise at work in the attempt to cognize, the efforts toward an epistemology quickly lead to a self-contradictory agnosticism, after which the undertaking is soon abandoned. Thinking realizes — though this does not happen consciously in thinking — that any statement it makes about itself can have no more value than any statement it makes about anything else. Thinking does not "see" itself while thinking, but only *after* thinking, after what has been thought; for the plane of thinking, of cognizing, is in no way altered by the fact that thinking thinks about what has been thought. Two philosophers are exceptions: Hegel and Gentile. Both have an intuition of the thinking process and place it in the center of their investigations, but neither is able to *experience* this process and provide guidance toward this experience. Rudolf Steiner assumed this task as his lifework.

THE CHALLENGE: TO EXPERIENCE
THE PROCESS OF THINKING

Based on the discussion so far, if we are to achieve an effective epistemology that does not succumb to these difficulties, the thinking process itself must be brought into the realm of experience. It is very clear this can be no mere speculation or further "reflection" but rather an action in its own right: a "doing."

Actually, every science, and particularly the natural sciences, should face this necessity. After all, we do everything, even all research, by means of thinking. But we really know nothing about the act of thinking. Should we not then know the tool with which we bring about everything—even technology? An often unconscious obstacle standing in the way of this challenge is that a new capability must be acquired, somewhat like achieving mastery in an artistic pursuit through doing and practice, rather than through reading, reflecting and gathering knowledge. Other than in the work of Rudolf Steiner, it is difficult to find guidance (pedagogy) for such an activity. Steiner's work, however, is not easily accessible for us today and remains unique in its approach and aim.

The consciousness soul provides the possibility for human freedom. This is demonstrated, for example, by the very fact that we can pose the question of freedom, which would be impossible if we were completely unfree. In that case we would not be able to grasp the concept of freedom at all, not even in our usual dull, half-conscious manner, because no authority, no organ in our being would notice the lack of freedom. To con-

ceive of freedom it is necessary to be aware of and attentive to the lack of freedom, as well as to be aware of
freedom itself. The human being must participate in
both.

The potential for freedom is inherent in the consciousness soul insofar as it can observe its own past thinking.
This past does not compel directly: it is a dead world,
powerless, shadowy, and precisely for that reason observable. The observing authority is *always* present but
always enters consciousness only *afterwards*, in the next
moment: always in the past. For the potential for freedom to develop into the actuality of freedom, it is necessary that the authority judging the past take hold of and
experience itself in the present. Other than this there is
no subject "present" which could be free. Only consciousness of the present can be free. The "I" concept we
ordinarily have is in fact only a memory, a shadow,
something already thought: a memory of an intuition. It
follows from this that the second half of *The Philosophy
of Freedom* describes the step that brings observation
out of its "standing over against" what has been already
thought into experience, the direct participation in
thinking in the present. Observation must be directed to
living thinking and the experience of living thinking. Living thinking is the process or supersensory power out of
which the already-thought appears. What we usually call
thinking is really the appearance of past thoughts. It is as
if flowing water, during its course, turned into particles
of ice, and the only thing we noticed was the ever-in-
creasing number of ice crystals: past thoughts. It follows
that ordinary consciousness, grounded in what has been
already thought, cannot experience living thinking.

Compared to ordinary consciousness, living thinking is *preconscious*.

THE EXPERIENCE OF THE ACT OF THINKING

The addendum to the eighth chapter and the beginning of the ninth chapter of *The Philosophy of Freedom* concern themselves explicitly with the experience of living thinking. First, dead thinking is portrayed, then living thinking and the experience of the latter. I quote the critical sentences (emphasis is from the original):

> The difficulty of grasping the essential nature of thinking by observation lies in this, that it has all too easily eluded the introspecting soul by the time the soul tries to bring it into the focus of attention. Nothing then remains to be inspected but the lifeless abstraction, the corpse of living thinking. [Note that mention is again made of the difficulties in experiencing thinking in the present, but it is not set aside as impossible, as in the quotation from the third chapter.] If we only look at this abstraction, we may easily find ourselves compelled to enter into the mysticism of feeling or perhaps metaphysics of will, which, by contrast, appear so "full of life." We should then find it strange that anyone should expect to grasp the essence of reality in "mere thoughts." But if we once succeed in finding *life in thinking,* we shall know that swimming in mere feelings, or being intuitively aware of the will element, cannot even be compared with the inner wealth and self-contained yet ever active *experience* of this life of thinking, let alone ranked above it. . . . Will and feeling still fill the soul with warmth even when we live through the original event again in retrospect. Thinking all too readily leaves us cold in recollection; it is as if

the life of the soul had dried out. Yet this is really nothing but the strongly marked shadow of its real nature —
warm, luminous and immersed deeply in the
phenomena of the world. This immersion is brought
about by a power that flows through the activity of
thinking itself — this power is love in its spiritual form.
There are no grounds here for the objection that to discern love in the activity of thinking is to project into
thinking a feeling, namely love. In fact, this objection is
but a confirmation of what we have been saying. If we
turn towards thinking *in its essence* [i.e., the living, not
the past thinking], we find in it both feeling and will,
and these in the depths of their reality [feeling that perceives, will that perceives]; if we turn away from thinking towards "mere" feeling and will, we lose from these
their true reality. If we are ready to *experience* thinking
intuitively, we can also do justice to the experience of
feeling and will. . . .[7]

The attentive reader will realize that these sentences
do not deal with the observation of past thinking
(thoughts), but rather speak of the experience of present,
living thinking. This is also described in the beginning of
Chapter Nine, from another point of view:

A proper understanding of this observation [of the
relationship of cognizing man to the world] leads to the
insight that thinking can be *directly* discerned as a self-
contained entity [obviously, here also, we are dealing
with a new form of experience, not a "standing over
against"]. . . . When we observe our thinking, we live
during this observation directly within a self-
supporting, spiritual web of being. Indeed, we can even
say that if we would grasp the essential nature of spirit
in the form in which it presents itself *most immediately*

to man, we need only look at the self-sustaining activity
of thinking. . . .

   We [who penetrate and behold the essence of think-
ing] shall see in this element that appears in our consciousness as thinking, not a shadowy copy of some
reality, but a self-sustaining spiritual essence. And of
this we shall be able to say that it is brought into consciousness for us through *intuition*. *Intuition* is the conscious experience—in pure spirit—of a purely spiritual
content. Only through an intuition can the essence of
thinking be grasped.[8]

In contrast to what was said about it in the fifth chapter of *The Philosophy of Freedom*, intuition is here characterized as an "experience—in pure spirit—of a purely
spiritual content." With this, the challenge to experience
thinking in the present receives a more tangible form: it
is to experience the process of intuition, of which, ordinarily, only the result enters our consciousness.

But intuition means being inwardly present, in an
identity, and not "standing over against." This understanding from within can be grasped clearly in the intuition of the "I," as it can also be grasped in every original
intuitional experience. In apparently stark contrast to
the quotation from the third chapter, Rudolf Steiner describes this experience in the second addendum to the
chapter called "The Consequences of Monism":

   For although *on the one hand* intuitively experienced
   thinking is an active process taking place in the human
   spirit, *on the other hand* it is also a spiritual percept
   grasped without a physical sense organ. It is a percept
   in which the perceiver is himself active, and a self-activ-
   ity which is at the same time perceived. In intuitively

experienced thinking, man is carried into a spiritual
world also as a perceiver.[9]

The contrast with the assertion that "active production and its objective contemplation" are mutually exclusive could not be more decisive. In reality there is no
contradiction here at all, since intuitive experience is neither objective contemplation ("standing over against")
nor "observation" in the usual sense, but rather is presence, *presentness* in the activity, the unmediated experience from within. This presence, presentness *in* the
activity, is practiced in every artistic pursuit. The singer
does not wait until the sounds have died away to observe
and judge what has been sung. It would be much too late
then to notice a false note. He or she "hears" it in the
process, even *before* the sound is produced, from within.
(This is why one says, aptly, when someone cannot sing,
that he has no ear, although obviously one does not sing
with the ear.) To be present in the moment, *in* the act of
cognition, and not merely to wake up to what has been
already thought, is to experience intuition, not merely its
result. This transparency of the act of cognition itself,
this not-forgetting of the cognizing behind the cognized,
this not-remaining-hidden of the wellspring of cognition,
is at once the experience of living thinking and of the
true I which alone is capable of this experience.

Ego-consciousness, the everyday I, lives by grace of
thinking. It needs finished thoughts (finished perceptions) to exist as consciousness at all. It rests on what
has been represented, remembered, already thought and
perceived.

The true I-am needs no support, no grounding (no I

think, therefore . . .). For *who* would substantiate it? It is itself the ground of all grounding, of all proof and support.

THE SPIRIT-SELF

For ordinary consciousness, thinking is a phenomenon whose sources and origin lie *before* the thinking consciousness. In order to cognize thinking, one must first produce it, and this one can do without first consciously (by thinking) learning how to. Logic is an *a posteriori*, descriptive (not normative) discipline, which describes how I think. I could not produce or understand logic if I were unable to think logically to begin with. As obvious as this seems, it is always forgotten by logicians.

> Man does not determine beforehand the kind of correlations that will come about between his thoughts—this determination would in itself be a train of thought—he only provides the place where the connection between them can occur according to their content, which inherently contains their essence.[10]

Where and by what means do the finished thoughts of ordinary consciousness arise? The lifework of Rudolf Steiner serves to answer this question. In his *Theosophy*, the answer can be found in elementary form.

The organ for intellectual intuition is the core of man's being, called the spirit-self.

> In the same sense in which the revelation of the corporeal is called *sensation*, let the revelation of the spiritual be called *intuition*. Even the most simple thought contains intuition, because one cannot touch the thought

with the hands or see it with the eyes. Its revelation
must be received from the spirit through the "I.". . .

[As] there could be no color sensation without physical eyes, [so] there could be no intuitions without the
higher thinking of the spirit-self. As little as sensation
creates the plant in which color appears, does intuition
create the spiritual realities about which it is merely giving knowledge.[11]

"Higher thinking" means life in living, cosmic thinking, in which intuition (literally, "inner presence," *Dasein*) allows us to participate. Yet in the reflection of our
ordinary consciousness this participation turns into a
dead and therefore untrue mirror image of the living
idea.

The following remark shows that in experiencing intuition a suprarational stage of consciousness is in play:
"And actually, no one should confuse this world conception with that based on the direct experience of thinking
with mere rationalism."[12]

So it is not a question of thinking about thinking. This
is simply a step in the direction of the metamorphosis of
consciousness: a metamorphosis of a consciousness of
the past into a consciousness of the present.[13]

One might ask why the third chapter of *The Philosophy of Freedom* so emphatically asserts the impossibility
of observing thinking in the present, while the second
half of that work presupposes the experience of the
thinking process. The answer lies in the above explanation that the experience of thinking is no ordinary observation from without, but an inner experience, an
intuition experienced in its making. This distinction has
pedagogical value. It is a matter of emphasis. The *soul*,

even if it is the "highest manifestation" of the I—namely, the consciousness-soul—cannot *experience* the spiritual. At best, it can behold the spirit's undistorted mirror image. For only *spirit* can *experience* spirit—a finger pointing at the moon is not the moon. The human being must rise to his spirit-self, to the center of his being, his higher I, in order to discern the play of spirituality in everyday consciousness and to recognize the source of the thoughts he has thought: i.e., living thinking. He must consequently actualize—at least momentarily—his potential identity with the "organ" of intuition: higher thinking. In this way one can experience what one usually receives preconsciously through this organ. Precisely this, this being veiled and yet attainable through uncompelled inner deeds, is the secret of the human promise of freedom.

The Fundamental
Experience of The Spirit

IF observations are to be made on common human interests, on the meaning of human life and the world
process, or on the developmental needs of humanity and
individuals, then we must and can proceed only from the
standpoint and perspective of today's average human being, and everything worth saying must be formulated in
the language of everyday people. Otherwise there is no
possibility of the ordinary person approaching and following what is said. On the other hand, we are all, more
or less, ordinary people.

In this sense we can immediately establish that if a person exercises a minimum of sobriety or epistemological
self-awareness, he will certainly discover a most basic
truth which can be summed up concisely in the sentence:
*All our knowledge and information result from and are
generated by our activity of thinking and can only be retained, expressed and communicated in the form of
thoughts.*

One could perhaps counter that surely a "simple" perception can also provide information, and that in this
case no thinking activity accompanies its occurrence. Yet
only a slightly deeper observation shows that in every

perceptual process the content represented in the perception arises only through thinking, even if the thinking is unobserved. Without conceptual determinations that run their course quickly and lightly, and therefore without being noticed, one would simply not be able to perceive anything determinate.

Whoever observes the content of his consciousness can note that this consists exclusively only of elements which either are of a purely conceptual nature or are bound up with conceptual elements. Human consciousness is a thought-consciousness.

That the above holds true for sensory knowledge is immediately clear. But what about knowledge that is not directed toward sense objects? What happens to thinking in the striving after a supersensible knowledge?

The inability of objective thinking to grasp supersensible realities is obvious from humanity's historical experience. From the Scholastics to Kant to the appearance of the first epistemological works of Rudolf Steiner, an ever-wider cleft appeared between the world of the senses and the world of the spirit, between *cognition* which was directed merely at the sense world and *faith* which aimed at supersensible reality. German Idealism, including Baader and Stirner, was unable to bridge this gap. Indeed, it can be established as a fact that human thinking as it has developed is not in a position to penetrate into regions of the supersensible.

That cognition of the sensible world, in the form in which it exists today, is insufficient for human beings can be attested to and proven in many ways. One need only think of the global dangers, of the threat to the whole of humanity and of the individual's anxiety in the face of life. Given this, each individual must pose for himself the question of the sufficiency of his cognition, and in each case it is the individual himself who must answer. Indeed, one could also say that whoever poses the question has already answered it. This holds also for the possibility of leaving the area of the supersensible to something other than cognition. Anyone who wishes can do so. What is said here is intended for those who have found that they cannot do this. It could also be pointed out that cognition of the sensible world is *itself* very incomplete, despite technical advances. The phenomena of life completely elude knowledge, and fundamental concepts of physics like mass, force, energy and force field still await clear conceptual interpretation.

Thus human beings today find themselves, quite simply, compelled to enhance their faculties for knowledge — a venture which would be undertaken in a conscious and self-determined form for the first time in history. Until the present, the development of cognitive faculties occurred without the conscious decision of humanity, as if by a process of natural growth.

The kind of cognition we aspire to cannot be less clearly conscious than thinking: it must involve an increase, not a decrease, a conscious enhancement of clarity, not a return to a more dreamlike form of consciousness.

How can a person change himself? At what point can he take his being in hand in order to advance himself?

Everything that enters human consciousness is an end-product, finished, completed — the last phase of the process from which it arose. This holds for perceptions of the sensible world as well as for perceptions of the inner world, the phenomena of the life of feeling and will. Indeed, if we carefully observe our conceptual life, we notice that thoughts and concepts usually become conscious only when they are finished, when they are already crystallized. Yet there is a basic difference between thoughts and all other contents of consciousness. While these other contents are given to me as if from outside, without any contribution on my part, I feel myself to be the producer of my thoughts. In my thought world, I feel as if I were free in my activity. When a feeling or an impulse of will emerges, I can no longer change it; at most, I can direct its manner of expression. In its emerging I have no part. I cannot feel whatever I want. Thinking is different. I can behold it completely; the content of thinking is for me completely transparent, filled with light, while everything else has by comparison a dark, opaque side. I understand everything else with the aid of thinking. Thinking is the element of understanding.

I feel at home in this element. To say "I think" is fundamentally different from other assertions, such as "I walk," or "I eat," for if I do something other than thinking I can follow this act with my thinking: I know simultaneously that *I* am doing something. But with thinking, to begin with at least, that is not possible. A certain practice, cultivation or maturity is necessary for a person to be conscious of himself, that is, to maintain his thinking intact while experiencing a feeling. In the case of thinking, however, we are identified, completely one, with this *activity*, as a naive person is completely one with his joy or pain. This implies that in his emotional experiences the human being today is more or less present as a conscious subject. But in thinking he is much less so; he is identical with it.

There was a time in the history of humanity when the human being was one with his feeling life while he felt his thoughts to be coming from outside.

It is clear from all this that today's human being is closest to his center in thinking—hence the transparent clarity of this thinking. This sheds some light on the nature of this center—it must be of the same kind as thinking.

Everything that approaches me is finished, already-become, dead—since this is all that my consciousness can grasp. I perceive nothing living; life is imperceptible to me. That a flower lives is no perception; it is a judgment, a conclusion. I cannot distinguish artificial flowers, plants or fruits made of wax or paper, if skillfully made, from their living counterparts. Likewise, I would have to investigate a mechanically driven replica of an animal form in order to ascertain that it is not alive. I am even less able to distinguish a living seed from one that is not.

I stand over against all phenomena; I find myself outside them. They are objects for me; hence, I call my consciousness objective. This is not so with thinking. Without my contribution, it does not happen. I feel that I stand immediately behind my thinking, as subject. With regard to thinking I am not outside; thinking is not something over against me. Everything else I suffer. Of thinking, I am the source.

At this point, two questions arise: (1) Who am I really, that I feel and designate myself as the subject of thinking? (2) Could I also behold my thinking as I can behold my life of feelings? If so, then my I-feeling would have to struggle to free itself from thinking, to release itself from identification with thinking. In what would this I-feeling consist? I shall now pursue the first question.

The human being lives, acts and thinks, whether consciously expressed or felt in silence, as if he were saying: I am body, soul, sensation, action and thinking.

When a person speaks in this way, when he experiences himself in this way, he lives a contradiction. For I can only be I, not the one who feels himself to be all this, but the one who knows, thinks and utters all these assertions. I cannot point to something outside myself—be it spirit, body or soul—and say: I am that. For I can only be the one who says this. Speaking thus, I express and live a contradiction. But that is precisely what I do, wittingly or unwittingly, as a modern human being. I have no experience of my innermost being. This being is not conscious of itself; it takes itself to be something else, to be body, to be soul, but not to be an "I." For my current ego cannot at all imagine that something could exist without appearing to me as something currently perceptible. But all that I hold in this way to be my being are things; they are the not-I, the other. I identify myself with these. They function in such a way that the subject may identify itself with them and thus cognize itself as object, since to begin with it cannot view or cognize itself otherwise. In order to see itself, the subject at first needs a mirror. It views itself in this mirror, sees the image, and says: I am that. The sheaths of being—body, soul, thinking—are such mirror images. I take myself to be the image so long as I do not experience the contradiction of this view.

From the suffering that stems from this contradiction, I learn my lesson sooner or later. Then I know that I am not the mirror image, but the one who sees the mirror image, the one who knows himself in the mirror. Indeed, I am the one who places himself in contradiction and takes himself for the mirror image.

If my body consisted only of a single eye, I could not see "myself" (the supposed "me") without a real mirror. Then in order to reach self-consciousness, I really would need a mirror. In this mirror I would come to know myself as an image. Indeed, I could become convinced that I am the image, particularly if a demon continually held a mirror before me. I need no real mirror for this process because I already find the mirrors within myself in the form of sheaths. Our continually present mirror, which we always carry with us, is our body, our soul. In that mirror I perceive myself: in it is my self. I live accordingly, because my education and the level of development of today's humanity lead me to identify myself with these sheaths. After all, they belong to me much more intimately than any external mirror.

I am body, I am soul: these are thoughts. As long as I live in accordance with such thoughts without grasping them consciously within myself and expressing them, I live without obvious contradiction. I really am soul; I really am body. However, as soon as I think and express this, contradiction is born in me and becomes manifest. And this manifest contradiction sends me on the search.

I seek the true subject. An initial observation along the way is the following. I cannot in truth be a body, since a body does not speak, nor think, nor can it say, "I am." I cannot be soul or feeling life because feelings come and go; and they are as incapable as a body of saying, "I am." No more can a perception speak or think, or become of itself a thought—that is, lift itself into consciousness. It is *I* who make perceptions into thoughts and so lift them into consciousness.

I am not body, but the one who thinks this identity; I am not the mirror image, but the one who sees it.

The eye is necessary for seeing, yet the eye does not see. It is I who see what the eye mediates. The eye is an almost purely optical apparatus, lens and darkroom, that delivers an image, a reversed image. But someone in the darkroom must see this image.

Hence, pure thinking teaches me that behind all my activities, as their subject, I find my I. I can, however, point to nothing that would be the I, nothing that would be I-myself. For anything to which I could point would be something outside me—even if I were to point to something that was not sensible. The I, the center, is indemonstrable, is invisible in the higher sense. It cannot be seen; it is nothing that has been seen, because it is the seeing. Only the I itself can see.

I am not body; I am not feeling. Thinking stands closest to me, for I somehow bring it forth and it is "transparent" for me (as well as for other thinking beings). But as I look at thoughts, they are *before* me; they stand over against me, and what I can observe in them initially is completed, dead, past, like everything that is perceived. Therefore, it is Not-I. For I must recognize myself as the subject standing behind all my activities, as a persistent and continuing presence.

Thus, through pure thinking, observing thinking, I separate content after content from my real I. I shed sheath after sheath. And what remains is a nothing. I can at first neither give content to my I, nor find content in it, for everything seems to be outside it. The only thing I can say of it is that it *is*. It is the true subject, the point-shaped source of my actions and especially of my thoughts. Yet this source can at first only say of itself: I am.

The great spectrum of the world in which I have lived until now draws itself together into this single, extensionless point that is myself. This point has no volume or content aside from itself. Thus I discover that I can know nothing of my true subject through pure thinking. I can experience nothing of my center except one thing: that it is. This existing point is the source of my being and my consciousness. This nothing is my living core. But perhaps this seed may sprout. Perhaps the rays of the world-spectrum, which draw together and cross in this seed, may somewhere and somehow—certainly not through pure thinking—break forth from this center onto the other side of space, into the inner space of the world.

After I have made it clear to myself by pure thinking that my ordinary I-feeling is not really legitimate—one could even say it is a deception—and that I can legitimately find only a point of which I know nothing, for which I can find no content, as my center, I turn to the task of finding a content for it after all. Finding this center through pure thinking does not mean that I am in this center. I only know that this center exists. Now I would like to seek it itself. Until now I have felt myself as body, as soul and as thought: now I would like to experience myself as pure I, and not merely know about it. Simply knowing about it leaves me the same as I was.

Behind all my activities stands my center. I observe these activities with the help of thinking, which lies closest to me and also closest to the center. This is the reason thinking is so transparent for that center. I can observe everything with thinking—except thinking itself. When my thinking observes something else I am identical with this thinking, or at least I feel it to be so.

The thoughts and the concepts which I have formed, created and finished are one aspect; another is the process, the power, by which thoughts, concepts and ideas occur in me. Ordinary consciousness lives in thoughts, concepts and ideas, but the process by which these appear is as unclear and unconscious to consciousness as the emergence of other contents. Since we have discovered that thinking is the activity of which we may most rightfully consider ourselves the originator, it is natural that we should attempt to observe not merely the end product, but also the development, the process leading to the product. From concepts and ideas, therefore, we turn to the power that brings them forth and to the process of bringing them forth. Our center is the persistent presence. But in our consciousness only the past (the dead) appears. In observing the process of thinking we nevertheless approach something that is present, i.e., living.

It is clear that with the observation of thinking we touch upon the above-mentioned second task, namely, releasing our identification with thinking, and thereby making the center, which at first supported itself by thinking and which experienced its existence in thinking, self-supporting. In this way the center emerges as the subject also of thinking.

But this step toward the observation of thinking itself shakes the foundation of our consciousness. For to observe something with which one is at first identified means to loosen this identity. Indeed, to see or feel oneself as something different from the object to be observed is already to have accomplished the most important preparation for this step. In a complete identification with the object one would not be aware of the possibility of detaching oneself from this foundation: such an idea could not arise. This is the form of everyday consciousness. Either we stand completely outside the event, in which case we as mere spectators can observe it well, or we completely submerge in the event, in which case we are carried along by the world-stream; we are the event; we ourselves become joy or sorrow and do not observe. In the one instance we are indifferent, abstract observers; in the other, naive, natural experiencers of the events.

Viewed in this light, observation of one's own thinking creates significant difficulties. At first we can observe thinking only after the fact. That is, we can observe only past thinking, the footprints of thinking, the produced thoughts. It seems hopeless to undertake to produce and to observe at the same time — all the more as in this case the means of observation would be the same as its object, namely thinking. Furthermore, the subject of both activities would have to be the same. The possibility of an activity being simultaneously followed through observation may be illustrated with an analogy. When we go to the theater and see a drama that affects us deeply, stirring our innermost being, we are in a situation that corresponds to neither of the above-mentioned extremes. We are, to be sure, only spectators, but we are in no way left indifferent; otherwise there could be no effect (such as catharsis). On the other hand, although we are not detached spectators, we do not wholly submerge ourselves in the dramatic events; we remain spectators throughout. An action which exercises, for example, a purifying effect on the empathetic spectator would affect him quite differently if he had to experience it in reality. The stage takes upon itself the weight of the events which the subject would otherwise have to bear in life. Thus he retains the strength to remain conscious of his own identity in the events. He is the spectator and, to a certain extent, also the experiencer at the same time. Is not the cathartic effect attributable specifically to this situation? If one pursues this peculiarity of the theater further, one comes to philosophy and reaches a deeper understanding of artistic activity in general.

To be both a spectator and an experiencer at the same time is, so to speak, given to us in the theater and made easier through its external arrangements. With the observation of the thinking process the challenge is more difficult, for here one is not only the one who experiences, but also, simultaneously, the spectator and producer.

We shall not go now into the techniques of observing thinking, but shall only point out the most important characteristics and results of such exercises.

The observation of thinking occurs through no organ other than thinking itself. Thinking must become so strong and independent that it appears to the subject with the same character of reality as does any outward perception. This is achieved through exercises in concentration, as far as this is necessary (and for the majority of people today it is necessary). At the end of concentration there always stands a pure idea that has no immediate relationship to the world of perception. The purer (in the philosophical sense) and the more dematerialized the idea becomes, the more easily seen through, the more transparent it becomes to the subject and the fewer the elements of perception it carries. It is the latter that hide the process of thinking from thinking itself. They stand before thinking as impenetrable surfaces, although they are erected by thinking—by a thinking, of course, which expresses itself in the (sensory) world of perception. Impenetrability is a fundamental law of the sensory, material world. A thought (that is to say, something spiritual) is penetrable by thinking. It is precisely the transparency of the pure idea that does *not* conceal the process of ideation, and thereby allows the process itself to become accessible and observable for the subject.

This process of observation is fundamental from two points of view. First, through such efforts, which often take a long time, a *subject* is molded that does not identify itself with thinking. Hence it needs neither to disappear in thinking nor to support itself in thinking in order to be or to know about itself. Since this subject knows how to observe thinking, it is independent of thinking and thus has laid aside its last crutch, its last sheath. It supports itself on nothing; it *is*. It has existence in and for itself. It is a being. It is an I that knows about itself independent of body, soul or thinking, and hence is independent of these also. Even thinking is something external for this I. This I is not outside itself: it is an absolute beingness, a primal spirit-being, that draws its meaning out of itself. But because it is a living spirit-being (that is, wholly transparent to itself) it can call forth the dead, frozen spirituality of thoughts, concepts and ideas. Spirit is the element of understanding, of transparency. Already-formed thoughts are petrified spirit. Living spirit, the I, calls these forth and is the source and the gate out of which thoughts flow and coagulate. So, by observing thinking, our I celebrates the *primal deed of spirit*: it cognizes itself and thus creates itself. It sees itself as spirit which is of and through itself a conscious entity, for there is no unconscious spirit. Nature is sleeping (unconscious) spirit; hence it is not spirit, as we ourselves are not, so long as our center is unillumined. With the illumination of the central point in the circle of psychic processes arises the first seed of our higher, i.e., our true, I. Its distorted mirror image is our everyday I, our ego. What comes into appearance in this lightning flash needs no mirror in order to see and to know about itself. It is the spiritual self, the spirit-self.

The second point of view which distinguishes the fundamental character of this event lies in the fact that, with the observation of thinking, something living is perceived for the first time — life itself, not just its sensible effects. Concepts and thoughts are dead, crystallized spirit, end products. In (philosophical) intuition I experience the living, timeless lightning flash of life, from which concepts stem. This intuition is also the primal image (archetype) of all higher intuitions. The living element in thinking is not the concept, but the relationship between two concepts, the still-fluid state prior to thoughts (*Vorgedanklichkeit*) that gives birth to the thoughts. It is that supraconceptuality whose living totality breaks up and crystallizes into individual concepts.

I think — I know that I have thought — I think the knowledge that I have thought.

These thoughts, this sequence of thoughts, is broken up by minute intervals. This separation and binding is the essence of thinking because it makes up the unnoticed, unspoken relatedness of concepts: their hidden background. I ordinarily experience this only as a gap, an emptiness in time or the continuum in which thinking reveals itself. This experience of absence persists until I learn to observe thinking. Then this stillness, this silence of intervals between individual concepts, emerges before me as a living element in thinking, as the womb of thoughts.

Thinking as process is life, which I usually disdain to see. The power that allows concepts and ideas to appear in humanity is the same as the one that allows life to be life. The I, the true center of the human being, is made of this substance. It is the spiritual, primal substance of the world, of all being ("and without which nothing is made"). Therein lies the reason that I can see this world, even with ordinary thinking, which is the dead shadow of that spiritual life. "In Him was life, and the life was the light of men, and the light shone in the darkness."

Until now, I-feeling has consisted only of answers to stimuli, feelings, thoughts. I felt myself only insofar as I was stimulated to an answer, to a reaction. The ego found itself through its reactions. The I, however, needs nothing in order to feel and to see itself. It is absolute cognition, complete transparency (because it does no "standing over against")—the archetype of absolute intuitive cognition, wherein the subject sinks into the object. Yet this does not occur unconsciously, as in earlier stages of I-development, but arises simultaneously with the establishment of consciousness. And because the I now really *is*, it can fully communicate itself. Capable of surrender, it has something to surrender. It can consciously and fully immerse itself in what is to be cognized. The potential for cognizing love begins. Cognition and love are a single life-stream.

Abstract thoughts are cold, and awaken no feeling. Having purified themselves of natural feelings, they become the preliminary stage of pure thinking. Experienced thoughts are, conversely, at the same time feeling-experiences. Yet thought is not produced out of and through feeling. On the contrary, one has thoughts and these evoke a feeling through their inner content. Thinking, however, is experienced when it can observe itself. It is the perception of thinking that saves it from the abstractness into which it fell as a result of shedding sensual perceptions.

To have the world before it as an object was given naturally to humanity. Humanity felt the I set over against the not-I, the not-I which is the world. From this, humanity could learn to have a certain free relationship to the object, and so the cognizing subject was born. This experience occurred without individual initiative on the part of human beings. They were led to it by their own nature, because everything in and about them that was not formed in their consciousness was nature. The meaning of this process was to teach humanity a relationship, to teach it a certain movement in relation to the object—a free relationship, a mental, purely mental, relationship; an independence from the object, an active standing over against.

The true object, however, is thinking. But it is not a matter of thinking about thinking. One can also do that, of course, but one does not get anywhere that way, simply because one continues to think the same thinking on the same level. Under certain circumstances one can paint painting, yet it remains only painting. What we are speaking of is an observation, a perception, but not a sensory one. Without this, we remain caught in abstract (because perceptionless) thinking.

Through the experience of the I, we reach the first spiritual experience of modern man. Without this experience, the question "What is spirit?" is answered only inadequately, or not at all. For we picture something of which we have no experience according to the patterns of the experience we do possess. Therefore, the figurative and parabolic statements in the descriptions of the spiritual researcher are often misunderstood. So long as one imagines spirit, soul or the etheric connected with even a breath of substantiality, spatiality or temporality, one is far from understanding their true nature.

With the experience of one's own true I—and humanity is on the verge of becoming conscious of this experience—one experiences an existence which is purely spiritual, without any sort of "matter," an existence as insubstantial as the thought-world. By means of this I-experience, one avoids picturing the spiritual being spoken of by the spiritual researcher as spatial and substantial. On the other hand, one has a cognitive experience in which one does not stand over against the object. This "standing over against" was, after all, ingrained through cognition in the sensible world. It follows that this same cognition cannot continue to exist in the cognition of the spirit. Here there is no "standing over against," but only conscious self-surrender, conscious identity—penetration into the object of cognition and mutual interpenetration, as one knows the thoughts of another only when one thinks them through oneself so as to become one with them and make them one's own. One can only cognize the spiritual when one become one with it. Standing over against is appropriate only when dealing with objects, even inner sense objects. We cannot stand over against the spirit—it immediately becomes non-spirit. It is not outside us; if it were, it would be non-spirit (*Ungeist*).

From this it follows immediately that spiritual science is no thing, no object, no knowledge towards which one can set a course in order, perhaps, one day to reach it. If one believes this, one forgets the role one's own thinking, one's own spirit, plays in the matter. It is I, through my thinking, who choose spiritual science for myself. It is I, through my thinking, through my judgment, who find its assertions to be true—for who else would? Spiritual science is, or should be, pure activity, and moreover, experienced activity. It is no teaching, no doctrine. It is a possibility of modern humanity, which originates in living thinking, in the awakened, experienced core of being. Whoever studies or practices spiritual science must move from dialectical thinking—however subtle that may be—to spiritual experience. Otherwise everything remains pseudo knowledge, dogma or belief, which however fails to recognize itself as such, and therefore is unbelief: superstition. We are no mere spectators in the cognition of the spirit; we alone can dis-cover (*entdecken*) our own activity as spirit. Then, we can experience the objective spirituality of the world in this activity. Even today the writings of the spiritual researcher are (despite the greatest publicity) occult writings; one must possess the key to them.

This key is given through the observation of thinking as just described. That is, at least, a safe and sure way to get it. Normal thinking takes its cue from sensory perception. It moves spatially from concept to concept and needs time. In an idea-intuition, we sometimes experience the supratemporal, supraspatial lightning flash of living spirit. And often, what is imparted in the flash is worked out and expressed at length through thinking. This flash is a precursor from the atmosphere of the region where our I is at home. We approach this region in the observation of thinking.

Once humanity said, I think, therefore I am. A person felt his own being sheltered, anchored and preserved in thinking. But what of the person who is able to experience his I outside, i.e., independently, of this thinking? What does he say? He no longer needs any support in order to be. His essence, his own being, answers for itself— it is its own guarantor. Therefore he can say the primal word: I am.

Concentration and Contemplation

THE final goal of concentration is contemplation, the realization of a self that experiences its own thinking, i.e., that looks on its own thinking while producing it. This goal can be approached only in a roundabout way, because "thinking in itself" cannot initially appear since it is bound to a theme, and because the self is present initially only in its mirror image: in the representation of the I which, identified with its sheaths, is experienced as ego. The ego must think *something*. It cannot do so directly, however; it can only *think around* something. To be able to do that without becoming distracted is the first step of the following exercise.

We should choose a time for the exercise when we are most alert, rested, quiet and relaxed. This will be different for each individual. One ought therefore to take great care to find the best time during the course of the day or week. Sitting (not lying), uncramped, consciously relaxing tight muscles, matter-of-factly, without "a halo around the head," one should begin one's exercise, as if, for example, one were seating oneself at the piano to practice. (Only for the dilettante is art "holy." Because of his excessive awe, he achieves nothing of it.)

CONCENTRATION ON AN OBJECT

The object should be man-made, a simple thing, not a natural object (such as a plant), for one cannot at first penetrate the latter. Therefore only the created aspect of the object should be thought, not its materiality, which is nature. The object should be uninteresting and aesthetically indifferent, releasing no emotions, such as pleasure or displeasure. One should not look at it, but think about it. It is recommended that the eyes be closed. Looking at the object hinders concentration. The exercise is to be accomplished exclusively in thought.

Thoughts circle the object: form, color, construction, function, etc., are thought. The representation of the object is formed and described from memory. Thinking should not only be free from distracting thoughts, but also undisturbed by itself: what will be thought in the future should not cast its shadow before it; what has been thought once (yesterday) should not be repeated according to memory, for that would no longer be thinking. Thinking should proceed absolutely in the present and where possible (but this is almost unattainable) by constant willing from moment to moment with uniform intensity. Drawing on yesterday's thinking distracts and makes the exercise boring, so that after a few days one is inclined to change the theme. Recollecting what was once thought is not thinking. What was once thought is as much a distraction, when it returns, as anything else that does not stem from thinking willed in the present. One can think the same thing every day, without ever noting that it is the same. For everything else besides present thinking is forgotten; it does not exist.

The willing should not become cramped, since this immediately extinguishes thinking. Cramping occurs mostly when we try to fight off distractions. Therefore it is important initially to think a short, firmly contoured train of thought: "The spoon is silver. It has a handle and . . . it serves to. . . . It has been cast or pressed. . . ." Whenever distractions arise, one should try, without fighting them, to look straight through them at the theme. To struggle with distractions only places them directly in the center of consciousness, suppressing the chosen theme.

Distraction may also consist of "straying thoughts" when one digresses too far from the theme. If one notices this, one should stop and try to find the series of associations by which one strayed. If these can no longer be found, one simply returns to the theme. Distractions, disturbing thoughts and representations may appear *alongside* the desired train of thought. At first one should not try to ward them off but simply turn one's attention to the theme. If that does not work, one should look "over the shoulder of the disturbance" at the theme. If that still does not help, then one should look for a moment directly at the disturbing representation, and then return to the theme.

It is left up to each person's own discretion what techniques to use in mastering the disturbance. It is best, however, to continue, unconcerned, with one's thinking. If further distracting thoughts or representations arise in the mind, it does not matter. They diminish in time. (Every pianist can hit a false key. That is not so important! It is play in the noble sense.)

When one has come this far, the compass of the theme grows constantly smaller of its own accord. Thinking becomes more intensive. One no longer needs so much "stuff" in order to stay with the theme. This happens as if by itself. Thinking begins to live: the will, which at first *willed* thinking from without, begins to live in thinking as spontaneity and, by becoming one with thinking, transforms itself so as to allow thinking to "unroll" from within. From this moment on, the exercise is a joy, independently of whether it "succeeds" or not. An interrupted exercise can be of much value, for unification of thinking with willing occurs in single, timeless moments. Gradually, one no longer *wills*: one does it. It becomes a game. One does not *wish to play*; one *plays*. A "blissfulness" arises; everything becomes natural and unforced. This blissfulness, however, cannot be held on to; it is not a permanent condition that fills consciousness. That would distract one again. Only the theme exists—that is the ideal. The theme and only the theme is thought, and not, for example, the success or nonsuccess of the exercise. Even the instructions are not thought. "The more I notice what I do, the less I do it." Concentration achieves its own momentum.

Success in the exercise is really not as important as the exercise itself. A person with a "playful" attitude is more likely to succeed. If the disturbances which arise with thinking are intense and cannot be eliminated in any of the above ways, then one may reduce the exercise to a minimal duration—for example, to one minute or even half of a minute. As it gradually becomes possible to carry out the exercise with full concentration, the time may be expanded. All these indications are general; each person must glean his individual instructions from his own experience.

If the distractions consist of digressing from the theme and will not diminish, then one must take even smaller steps, shorter thoughts, thinking one thought, for example, twice. But one must *think*—not repeat.

The circle in which thinking moves around the theme grows ever smaller of its own accord; at the same time, thinking becomes more and more intensive, indeed, slower. This slowing-down proceeds correctly when one gives up verbal thinking. At first one thinks in words and representations. Then, as the exercise intensifies, one begins more and more to think the *theme* itself, not just the words and images. One must have a great deal of material for verbal thinking; otherwise it stops, because such thinking lasts only as long as one inwardly says or represents the words. The more abstract these are, the more quickly thinking stops. Therefore, to begin with, one should take not a concept (goodness, a triangle, etc.) as a theme, but a definite object (a spoon, for example, with a monogram). This object is described, represented and, where possible, inwardly seen; the same with all further thoughts that belong to it. In direct proportion to the intensification of the activity, the words fall away more and more. Thinking becomes more intensive, because it bases itself on less and less.

The discussion concerning the first stage can be extended almost infinitely. As a supplement, it is useful to retain in writing any new insights, referring to the technique, gained during the exercises. Thus, for example, a person may discover that he is inclined to think intermittently, rather than continuously; he thinks a "sentence" (that is, a motif), pauses and rests, and only then thinks a second. The danger is that one will be distracted during the "resting period." One must attempt to concentrate in a continuous movement; otherwise one easily drifts into a more or less disconnected series of images, thus, into nonthinking.

Some people are more inclined to think in pictures and representations, while others are inclined to think more abstractly. It is advisable to practice *both* sorts of concentration, switching daily; for example, one day more abstractly, the next more pictorially. The pictorial thus serves as a preliminary stage to Imagination, while the abstract (nonpictorial) comes into its own in the second stage of concentration.

When the exercise goes well, and one has already taken pleasure in it, is no longer bored and can hold the representation without thinking too many words, one can proceed to the second half or second stage of the exercise. The first stage is quite complete in itself, and with intense practice one advances spontaneously.

BEHOLDING THE IDEA

The second stage of concentration grows in uninterrupted progression out of the first. Namely, if the possibility of reducing the circle of thoughts presents itself, then one can consciously help it along. Out of the object of concentration one makes a pure idea or a pure concept. This means a concept which contains no elements of representation or perception, but is rather the "common" element wherein and whereby we "know" that all corresponding individual sensible objects belong to this concept. If we take, for example, a drinking glass as a theme for the first stage of concentration, then the second stage would begin when, by thinking or representing, we produce many possible versions of the glass before us, from chalice to liqueur glass perhaps, in order to grasp the common element of all these individual specimens. Only this "common element" gives us the right to designate each of the different examples, despite their differences, as a "glass." All of us have actually at one time unconsciously experienced this concept or idea in our childhood. Now, however, this can take place consciously. This idea contains no elements of perception, for these belong to the individual glasses.

From now on, this pure idea becomes the theme of concentration. Obviously it is formed initially through verbal thinking, but as an idea it is no longer something verbal. It is more nearly a picture, though not one that would resemble a sensory perception. Idea and picture are one at this stage, as they *originally* were, namely, at the first production, the first creation of a glass. As intuition, concept and picture, idea and representation were undivided. It is the same with all original, fundamental "inventions," as well as with children's (and sometimes adults') cognitive intuitions.

As the theme of concentration, the idea won in this way has two important properties. One is that it is "transparent" to thinking, like a mathematical formula or a geometric figure. A perceptual representation (the individual glass) is never wholly transparent to thinking, and therefore is a perception, not a concept or an idea. A representation "covers up" the thinking process. But a pure idea "is" this thinking process itself. The second property of an idea is that it is never "finished": it leaves nothing dead behind it. Only because an idea-picture is continuously produced is it present in consciousness. The idea exists only in the process of its original begetting. Representation happens quite differently. It is called into consciousness as a memory picture, where it can be observed. The intensive activity required for the generation and production of an idea is not needed for this. The pure idea is always a flow, a stream of thinking. It is a streaming, like light or music. Therefore, one can say; theme and thinking have become one. Theme does not exist outside thinking. Insofar as one concentrates on the theme, one beholds simultaneously one's own thinking activity.

One should concentrate throughout only on the theme. The thought, "Now I am observing my thought activity" should not arise, for that is no longer thinking the theme. Consequently, there could be nothing there for one to observe. In time, the realization dawns by itself that this concentration is *at the same time* the experiencing, the living of the thinking process. It is "observation" only in a figurative sense; it is not observation from outside, not standing over against. Neither the theme nor the thinking itself is an "object." It is the living experience of thinking in the present and at the same time the birth of one's true I or spiritual self: the spirit-self. For whoever is capable of experiencing his own thinking process is present independent of this thinking. This consciousness does not support itself on thinking, on the already thought ("I think, therefore I am"), but can exist alongside thinking. Ordinary consciousness (ego, everyday I) lives by the grace of thinking, but the consciousness that is now attained is the *source* of thinking, the true I-am.

In the practice of the second stage, one may take a new theme, for example, the pure concept of triangle or circle. Nevertheless, in the beginning it is better if one takes the theme that was the basis of the first stage, rendering it "sense-free." For in this way the power with which one built the representation and thoughts of the first stage can live on, metamorphosed, in the second.

The living experience of thinking leads to the experience of so-called living thinking. This is the element prior to thought, the sphere from which thoughts stem. It may be compared to the fluid that still contains in suspended form the solid particles which will later crystallize. To experience this sphere, at least to approach it, is of fundamental importance, for it is the first experience of the supersensible: the sphere of the Etheric. One sees that this is nothing spatial, material or substantial. It is a sphere of *being*, previously unknown to consciousness, but which now bestows on the latter an inner, absolute certainty—a living experience that shatters and blesses. Therefore one does well *not* to live the shattering and blessing during the exercise, nor to *want to* enjoy or even take notice of it, but to continue steadfastly with the exercise.

From the beginning of the first stage until the end of the second stage, the task is always one and the same: to concentrate oneself. Everything else, even the possibility of continuing beyond the second stage of concentration, really happens of its own accord.

The second stage is clearly even more susceptible to distraction and digression than the first, because in it the theme exists only through one's own activity. Dependence on any concrete existing thing ceases. Therefore, concentration and the avoidance of distractions must be practiced and strengthened in the first stage.

The second stage works *indirectly* on the whole soul-life. With the birth (awakening into consciousness) of the true self, ego-feeling becomes more and more super-fluous. Feeling becomes free. Feeling becomes cognizing once more. It begins to feel as seeing sees. The will, already strongly involved in the first stage of the exercise, now experiences a further purification. Self-will becomes superfluous, because the I needs nothing in order to assert itself. *It is*, i.e., "I am," whereas the ego asserts its existence, its consciousness, only out of its self-will, its self-feeling. The I does not assert itself, indeed, *it does not cognize itself* (who is to cognize whom?); it *is*, absolutely. Cognizing and being come together in it. It is absolute tranquility, and at the same moment it is greatest activity. It does not think, does not feel, does not will; it is simply there, no more, no less. Therefore it is called the fundamental experience of spirit.

When the same conduct, stance, attitude, that was reached in concentration is applied to the world of perception, one achieves pure perception, or the Goethean "visual power of judgment" (*anschauende Urteilskraft*). By means of the latter, one receives the conceptual aspect of the world of perception through perceiving, not through thinking. Ordinary thinking remains silent. Living thinking is always alert and ready, it is present. It is cosmic (nonsubjective) thinking, the essence of the world of perception. It is the Reality of the World.[1]

In the second stage of concentration one already gradually approaches unmediated cognition. All cognition is usually mediated through thinking, representation or perception. In the final analysis, however, all cognition rests on immediacy; it is a becoming aware, an understanding, without words or concepts, without knowledge. Such is the place of meditation.[2]

DIFFICULTIES

It may happen during the exercise that consciousness sinks into half-dreaming. When this is noticed, it is well to break off in order to begin anew and repeat the exercise in a more favorable, more wakeful condition, for the desired state of consciousness is definitely on a *higher* level than the ordinary degree of wakefulness.

It may also happen that, in pictorial representation, the object of concentration begins to live on its own — that is, to move, change, shift colors, or become "beautiful" or "ugly." The basic characteristic here is that the *object* itself lives. The person doing the exercise does not move the object; he only observes the changes that the object goes through independently of him. With diligent attention, however, we can always discover that though indeed we represent the object pictorially, we then place this representation fixedly before us. The object was, to be sure, not physically given. We "observed" its representation, but we did not actively think it. The attention directed toward the representation becomes fixed, and, in comparison to thinking, passive. When the fixed attention has sufficiently concentrated, then the will — itself concentrated in the attention and thereby condemned to passivity — goes over into the image of the object. The image thereby awakens to life. What is described here is a kind of straying from the purpose. We gaze in a passive way on the object, which has become "independent." Thoughts and representations, however, must always be created actively by us.

Another difficulty has already been mentioned. It is very hard to free oneself from the memory of a course of thoughts once run through, and because of that, concentration can change into remembering. Clearly this is another very disturbing distraction, particularly in the beginning. One is then inclined to change the theme, but soon the same thing will happen with the new theme. Therefore, it is advisable to remain with the "boring" old theme, and to overcome the difficulty from the ground up. Concentration is completely independent of the novelty or age of the theme. In fact, it succeeds better if the thoughts are known. However, they may not be taken from memory. The advice to exclude memory, to forget the already-thought, is easily given but very difficult to follow.

When we first begin to exercise, it is not easy to achieve undivided attention. We are demanding something out of the ordinary from our attention: to occupy itself with something in which it has no interest. In such cases the attention must be *willed*. Thus we may feel two subjects in us at the same time: one that is *attentive*, and another that *wills this*. When this happens, the memory can easily disturb the "subject that wills," for the latter finds it easier to remember than to think.

The problem is really this: How to begin, when, as yet, no pleasure results? One must will, and this willing distracts from the doing. But how do willing and doing become one? How can one fuse the "two subjects"? As far as beginning is concerned, we can proceed by inserting a waiting period before beginning. We sit down and wait until the ever-present, restless agitations subside. When the problem, "Shall I do it or shall I not?" is present in all clarity, we simply turn to the theme and begin the exercise. If the "two subjects" still emerge at the beginning, then we *do not begin*. This not-beginning can be repeated a few times. After that, things will usually improve. Another possibility is to tell the sequence of thoughts in one's concentration to an imaginary person, which at least slows down thinking to the speed of speech and, furthermore, helps one to forget the "two subjects" and to unite willing and doing.

The presence of the two subjects means basically that we are *not yet really thinking*. Stated more exactly, we practice the same sort of non-thinking that is normally called thinking; i.e., we think *about* something, not *this* thing *itself*. Ordinarily, we do not think the object itself, but rather the thought about it that we have formed at some other time. Or we think the already-once-formed representation, instead of forming it only now. We do not actualize being-with-the-object; rather, we think about its representation. More exactly, we call forth into our memory representations and thoughts about the object. We do not stand and confront the object (the theme) as we did the first time. In the extreme case, this non-thinking can become simply verbalism, mere words called into memory.

Real thinking is the complete unity of thinking and thinking-willing, so that a twofold "presence" cannot even emerge. It is a matter not of repeating representations and thoughts out of memory, but of continually thinking anew, independent of whether the thoughts are new or not. Even thoughts that have already been thought can still be thought anew, with the same intensity and exclusive attention as the first time. When we speak of the concentration of thought, we mean this real and present thinking. It could also be described as a continual condition of "understanding"—here, there is no question of a memory-like repetition. It is a constant being-present with the theme—the greatest possible identity with it. One understands from this what real thinking is, and how it differs from merely fetching up what has already been thought and already been represented.

In the event that initial difficulties concerning the will have now been overcome, one can avoid the theme's becoming boring by concentrating representationally (and not in abstract thoughts), thus slowing down the process. In this way not so much "stuff" is needed. This succeeds all the sooner and persists all the longer in proportion to the detail in which the representational images are worked out (the more, for instance, each tooth of a comb is individually carved out in the representation).

In order to characterize the will needed for concentration, consider the following image. Picture a state of complete physical exhaustion. Physical vitality is exhausted to the point where you are incapable of any activity, of any act of will. You can only lie there, motionless. If you nevertheless must do something, then somehow you bring forth a will to do this act. *This* will, however, does not come from the physical body, since the body is exhausted. It is this same will that you bring forth in concentration—or in any artistic activity (naturally without supposing physical exhaustion).

In the first stage of concentration, it is helpful for the success of the exercise to mark out the compass of the theme in advance in order not to stray too far from it. One limits oneself, for example, to (1) form and color; (2) construction; (3) function or application. With this third step, one passes to the second stage, for the function usually does not belong solely to an individual object.

Self-observation in either stage of concentration is a dangerous distraction.

In case it is too difficult to exclude from consciousness the effect of noises coming from our surroundings, it sometimes helps to direct our attention to the murmur of stillness. In complete silence this murmur is easily noticeable: it is a soft sound caused by the circulation of blood in the ear. Hearing this murmur, we are no longer disturbed by other noises, for it is the softest and innermost noise. Through a little practice we can hear it even in the presence of louder noises. If one succeeds in this, then it is only a question of putting aside this one disturbance, of leading the attention from it to the theme of the concentration. Perceiving the murmur of silence is a transition point into the security of undisturbed being.

The Boundaries
of the Soul

YOU ASK concerning the human image: What is man? So posed, the question is deceptive, and the answer inevitably fails to do justice to the human being. For the human being himself is the questioner and the object of the question, and therefore a *who* and not a *what*. The question can only be: *Who* is man? And the answer must come directly from this experience itself. The human being questions, and the human being answers.

No other being has questions, only the human being. Beings of nature—rocks, plants, animals—do not question. The animal knows the answer in advance, before the question; therefore it is no answer. The animal is not questioned; it can only react. The human being is questioned, placed in question. By whom? By himself. For the human being the world is questionable, and he thereby becomes questionable to himself as well. Answering is not reacting.

In asking and in answering, one becomes human. *This* is the human being: the openness to being addressed actualizing itself in questioning and answering. In understanding the question one is human; otherwise there is no question. In understanding the answer, one is human; otherwise there is no answer. But not understanding, not answering, is human too—exclusively human. Whether one speaks or is silent, whether one comprehends or does not—even in the denial of his humanity, one is always the human being.

To the degree that there are beings higher than humanity—and everything not humanly created testifies to a cognizing and being cognized—they must stand completely within cognition, otherwise they would be human. These beings have no questions; they can only ascend from cognition to more illumined cognition, or immerse themselves in ever-brighter light. Only humanity knows the gloom of the question and the joy of the answer.

The human being has his world and is in his world. What the human being is not is his world, which is always the world that he has cognized. It is a provisional world, but he does not think about that. For him, it is solid enough, objective—his opposite. The inner structure of his questioning is conditioned by his being woven into this world in a threefold way.[1] In that he is *body*, the world is given to him through his sense organs. In that he is *soul*, joy, pain, sympathy, hate arise in him through the world. In that he is *spirit*, he cognizes the world. To cognize is more than a subjective feeling: the world is truly *thus*. The body is the world for the soul. The world as something cognizable or cognized is the world for the soul. The *soul* cognizes body as body and cognizes itself through the powers of cognition, the spiritual powers, that it possesses. With these powers it can also cognize spirit, cognition itself. But this cognition is obscured by the use of the cognitive powers which illumine the cognized. In order for cognition to appear, there must be someone present for whom it can appear.

The structure of the question is conditioned by the fact that soul is not spirit, is not-cognizing. As soul, it is precisely that which does not cognize, although it has the potential for cognition: spiritual powers. The soul is not-world: the world is always cognized; the soul is what is separated from the world. The separation itself, the not-cognition, the boundary of the world, is the soul. The boundaries of the soul are the soul itself. Hence, darkness.

Not wholly darkness, not wholly light. A darkness in which light can shine, but a darkness that defends its own boundaries. In the play of light and darkness arises the world of color, and in the play of sense and deafness, the world of sound arises. The soul is the questioner, the soul is the answerer, and the powers of questioning and the powers of answering are spiritual powers: powers of the Logos; powers that have built the world, for it is a cognizable world; powers that are active in the soul, for the soul can cognize the world.

> When the soul speaks, the spirit speaks through the soul.
> When the soul is silent, the spirit is silent through the soul.
> The soul is the spirit's dark veil.

Heraclitus speaks: In all your wandering, though you travel every path you will never find the boundaries of the soul—so deep a Logos does it have. He also says: The soul has a Logos which increases itself. Of the

Logos he says: Although the Logos is common to all, most people live as if they had individual thinking. What they continually encounter, the Logos, they divorce themselves from, and what they stumble over daily appears alien to them. For everything happens according to this Logos. . . .

The boundaries of the soul are the boundaries of cognition. If the soul were entirely windowless, there would be no cognizing, and it would be no soul, because it could not distinguish itself. But where there are boundaries *and* windows, there is twilight and dawn, sensitivity and awareness of sensitivity. Because the sensitivity is noticed, it is not the sensitivity of the animal. It can be an organ of cognition, but it can also serve to feel itself.

To have boundaries means to have surfaces; means sensitivity; means the need for movement for the sake of friction, because surface senses surface through friction. This is self-sensing, not cognizing.

Cognizing is reading; reading in the physiognomy of the cognized, not friction. The surface must be there for cognition to be necessary, for it to occur and for there to be a cognizer, but cognizing does not occur by means of the surface.

The soul can cognize, but it prefers to sense itself on the surface. The surface is the boundary of the world. To cling to the surface is to cling to the world. It is to defend the surface, to long for the world, to long for longing, to desire desire.

Pleasure and pain are surface reactions. They serve self-sensing. But pain can lead the soul out of longing for longing.

Boundaries, clinging, desire, pain, self-feeling and wanting-to-feel-itself: soul. This is the property of the soul; it is "its own." It is the soul's error to believe that it is this—this property. Only slowly does the soul begin to seek the one to whom all belongs.

The soul's first answer is: I am body. It feels itself bound to the body. It knows its dependence on the body. But where it is aware of the dependence, it must be independent; otherwise it would not notice the dependence, and would always go along with the body totally. The soul must be in some way autonomous, or it could not demonstrate its independence.

Just open your mouth to speak: you have made a declaration of independence. And when you are silent, that too is a silence born out of freedom. The human being is not free, but he knows about freedom, and in that he is free. If one were totally unfree, he would not know about it. If one were totally free, he would not know unfreedom; nor would he notice freedom; he would not be free. A share in freedom, a share in unfreedom: that is human freedom.

That the body is, is a determination, a cognition of the soul, through the spirit. Even soul and spirit are cognitions of the spirit in the soul.

It can occur that the soul sees or thinks or perceives: that it cognizes. It can turn itself to the cognitive powers. The cognitive powers cannot derive from the cognized world, the "small" world in which cognition itself neither appears nor is a reality. This is our ordinary world picture, concrete and objective, but within it cognition is not a reality, because this picture represents the already-cognized world.

But cognition *is*, otherwise the world picture would not exist. Cognition is in the world, for where else would it be? *That* is the world, the great world, where cognition has its place. But the human being at first knows only the small world: his world.

The cognitive powers are unknown to the soul. It uses them without experiencing whence they come. For only the cognized becomes conscious — what has been thought, what has been perceived. Cognition itself precedes these; it is preconscious. Consciousness arises with the cognized, through the cognized. Ultimately, understanding is always immediate. After long chains of mediations, transformations, finally one understands. After the last mediation. That is immediate cognition. One could assume that the cognitive powers are impersonal powers, that intuition comes from an impersonal world, that of ideas perhaps. But the first intuition of self-consciousness is the intuition: I. Consciousness of self is only present *after* this intuition. So the source must be personal. Intuition understands itself, nothing else; only later does it re-cognize itself in the other — which then is no longer an other. The source is the *I am*.

Consciousness does not see through itself; it is impenetrable for itself. It is not self-supporting. When we wake up, *we* do not do it; after we have awakened, our consciousness is there. Consciousness does not cause awakening.

At every moment, the soul is nourished by the spirit, which at first the soul does not know. The spirit does not know itself; it is cognition itself. The source of knowing, of cognizing, is the spiritual self: boundless.

The primal phenomenon is cognition. It "is" only in terms of itself. Existence, understanding, is what it consists of: absolute transparency. Everything we know, about which we know, is cognized. The primal phenomenon is called spirit.

Whatever the soul cognizes, to that it surrenders. In surrendering it knows nothing of itself. In not-cognizing it awakens. In surrendering, in understanding, it sleeps. In self-consciousness it is awake, present to itself. The one who thinks is the I; the one who has thought is the soul. The soul oscillates between cognizing sleep and not-cognizing waking consciousness. Therefore, the soul has no present.

What becomes conscious is past, is surrender to the world, surrender to the body. At one time, in childhood, the soul identifies itself with the body. Thereafter it says "I" to the body — an intuition arising in it at the moment when it binds itself to what was, and still is, being built by the I, but is not the I, yet is the I's own other.

The link to the body hinders the act of surrender to the world. The soul's cognitive powers are the leftover cognitive powers, the remnants. In this way, the external, the internal, the boundary, the soul itself, arises. The garment. At every moment the soul sleeps, the soul awakens.

The soul's autonomy rests in its spiritual power, the power of attention. Attention is mostly put in the service of wanting-to-feel-itself, but the soul can become aware that it has the power of attention. The soul can desire this power for its own sake, without an object—as pure power, as possibility, as preparedness.

The process begins with the concentration of this power on something that is unimportant and uninteresting. Attention to such a representation can be intensified to an infinite degree. The scattered forces that ordinarily flow between the lines of life,[2] themselves appear. First focused on something unimportant, then concentrated on a pure idea, finally attention without an object appears. Attention is withdrawn from the body—even a physical pain can disappear through concentration on something else. The soul lives attention without object; thereby it experiences itself without any "something else." It becomes present to itself without the past, without what has been thought, without what has been perceived; it becomes pure presence— for the first time it becomes life.

The need to move ceases. This is the inner quiet of the sea. The soul cognizes the core of its being, its spiritual self. The soul becomes the source of cognition. It no longer needs boundaries in order to be.

The first boundary is what has been thought,[3] mirrored consciousness. Dead, because mirrored; abstract, because dead. To live in thinking instead of to live dying in what has been thought; to experience conceiving instead of merely the concept: such is self-cognition. Otherwise everything remains what has been thought. Whether "spirit" or "matter" is what has been thought, insofar as it has been thought, it is all the same. The first boundary is the boundary of what has been thought. It is the boundary of life. That is why man does not know life.

In travelling *all* the paths, in going the ways of cognizing, you no longer find the boundaries of the soul — so deep is its Logos. But the soul must reach its boundaries for these to vanish. The boundaries of the world are always within the soul.[4] The Logos in the soul, the soul experiencing itself, increases through itself. What is not yet, arises. Soul becomes spirit, or spirit becomes soul: the human being.

Truth is the sublation of forgetfulness, a re-establishment of what always is, and is only concealed by the boundaries, by the soul.

Truth is event, deed, praxis. It cannot be a possession, any more than music can. What is truth?

The way is truth. Life is truth.

Becoming true and becoming aware: there is no other competence. Whoever asks is not in the truth. His question is the truth, veiled. Likewise the act of questioning itself. No truth can be proved. No truth needs proof. It shines. The ultimate truth is a smile between God and humanity: between divinity and divinity.

The Secret of Perceiving

A FTER ALL, the world is always the seen world. There is no seen without seeing, no seeing without a seer. That ought to be enough for us to cognize the "little world" as *our* world. But ordinary consciousness lacks this cognition. To this consciousness, the world seems just to "be there"—perhaps not exactly as it appears to us, but in any case, *independent* of us. As cognizers we do not belong to it. The notion that something can "be " without being cognized is the central superstition of our times, although, in fact, the "little world" can certainly be recognized as our own product. This superstition is nourished by so-called idealism, which maintains that the whole world picture is only a product of consciousness. And by "consciousness" is understood ordinary consciousness: the very one which arises only *after* perception, *after* thinking.

In reality what appears in consciousness is a picture, i.e., no longer the world itself. Realism circumvents this difficulty with the analogy of reflection: the picture *in* consciousness is the objective mirror image of an objective reality. Kant formulated it radically: What I know is already within; of what is without I can know nothing immediately.

But ordinary consciousness is not concerned with the assertions of philosophers. To the unreflective person the world as it appears feels solidly objective, independent of cognition. And this feeling cannot be changed by the thought that the world picture must somehow be given to consciousness for the problem to be discussable at all. This feeling belongs to consciousness; actually it forms ordinary consciousness. No thought process can disturb it. Because this picture of the world is not changeable through an act of consciousness, all talk of the picturing activity of ordinary consciousness falls by the wayside. It can do nothing to the world picture. It can be a faithful or an unfaithful mirror, but it cannot account for itself. In all its movements, it rises out of preconsciousness, in which it is rooted. It experiences neither its own arising nor any creative movement. Only afterwards can it register the results of what has gone before.

While I am asleep, this world does not exist for my consciousness. The world sets with my consciousness; the two processes are inseparable. And when I have awakened, I discover that during my sleep "someone" guaranteed the continuity of my consciousness. The same may be said of the continuity of the world picture. It also was guaranteed. In this way consciousness on the one hand and the world picture on the other come and go always at the same time. Neither precedes the other.

When I think about awakening, I can say that my consciousness exists objectively, i.e., independently of me. After sleep, consciousness surfaces from what preceded it. It becomes "consciousness" only afterwards.

But sleep and this surfacing also occur during wakefulness. When I perceive a flower, I am totally with it in my attention; I am the flower. I do not think, "I am the flower," but I behold, see, think, the flower. Thereby I am the flower. Then I "wake up" and say, "There is the flower," or "I see the flower." But now I no longer see it. I know that I have seen it, that it is there. But I am here, with myself. I am awake. I am with my consciousness. But while I was with the flower in perceiving, my continuity was preserved, just as it was at night in sleep. I can return.

I experience thinking as an activity in which I am totally involved. This experience is only appearance; I do not ordinarily experience thinking at all, only what has been thought. Furthermore, when I think, I constantly touch the region of sleep. Whence comes what has been thought?; whence is dialectic nourished? An unconscious wellspring must exist: the power of the Logos in me. Where this power or the movement brought about by this power stops, however, precisely there my consciousness awakens. It catches sight of itself: what has been thought stands there, represented. It seldom happens that I glimpse that source directly. In this rare and exceptional situation, the source appears as a foreign authority. For my self-consciousness is, to begin with, at home only where this power disappears in its product. My self-consciousness flashes up precisely through the extinction of this power. This flashing up reveals a twofold process. I could not endure the power itself; it would destroy me as a separate self.

I designate as the inward the direction from which my thought thinking appears. The direction from which I sense the power of mental intuition I call the outward. In perceiving, I experience myself as passive. Although the perceptual pictures doubtless appear "within," I experience these pictures as if they had come about without my contribution. This experience of foreignness is not at all affected by the fact that every perceptual picture is woven through with conceptuality, i.e., is simultaneously thought. My experienced passivity lends these pictures their experienced objectivity. Thus, the world of perceptions appears to be numinous—like a divinity. It appears to be there without my contribution, independent of me. My self-consciousness arises solely because I can withdraw myself both from perceiving and from thinking something, and can reassure myself that *I* have perceived, *I* have thought. I can withdraw myself from all states of surrender. I recall the activities which I really become aware of only through their results. I sense them only behind the scenes of the perceived and thought, which appear on the stage of my attention.

Everything discussed so far is cognizing. Nothing would exist for us without cognition. In the beginning is cognizing. Nothing more fundamental can exist as the source of all statements concerning perception and thinking.

Insofar as a person today forgets his own role in thinking and perceiving, he acts irrationally. Nor is this forgetfulness something innocent and fortuitous. Were one to give up this forgetfulness, he would face the task of altering his whole world picture, hence his culture and his social institutions. Above all, however, one would have to change oneself. That is why we do not ascribe cognizing itself to the world of reality! The element, through which we cognize all realities!

In search of an explanation of perception, the psychologist and physicist seek a "medium" that is itself imperceptible. In doing so they behave logically. The process of perception cannot be experienced; otherwise it would lead perception back to new, further perceiving, to other perceptions. The researcher wants to avoid this but does not notice that his principles, which are not directly perceivable (waves, oscillations, photons, nerve-complexes, etc.), also enter consciousness only through perceptions—indeed, much more complicated and demanding perceptions than those he wishes to explain.

It is hard for us to understand that thinking and perceiving are, in the final analysis, immediate. Yet in unmediated cognition, without a "foreign" medium, the reality of spirit holds sway. Cognition cannot be traced to something that is not cognized. Every explanation of cognizing presupposes this very thing. The question thus becomes more pressing: what hinders us in that cognition, which is always present as a possibility?

The boundaries of the soul both hinder cognition and make it possible. The soul is placed between the world and the spirit; thus between spirit and spirit. Hence the soul establishes the boundaries. The homogenous stream of cognition is interrupted, divided in two. The universal world process appears from "within" as thinking, from "without" as perceiving. The soul has separated out—"given birth to"—the manifestation of the conceptual. From this part it has built an inner world. Originally, life was created in this ideal element. Not yet biological life, but living standing-within the stream of the cosmos, cognizing standing-within the waves of the world: living idea, cognizing feeling, cognizing, identity-bearing will.

When the cosmos fragmented, feeling and will, originally cognitive powers, became the building blocks for the boundary experiences of the soul. Instincts now adhered to the surfaces of the world, without any inner disclosure of their essence. Desiring and lacking, soul-surface gropes towards fragments of world-surface. From the leftovers of the cosmos perception arose.

Yet the soul's boundaries do not imprison it; it is not windowless. The senses are permeable; the whole meaning of the world streams through the senses. The senses do not cognize — they offer no resistance. They are selfless and do not affect perception. The soul cognizes. And in order to experience itself in perception, it dampens down to almost total lifelessness the life streaming through the senses. This dampening down does not occur consciously. The soul only knows: *there* is the world, *here* am I.

On the other hand, by means of all that was thought the soul constantly blocks its access to the world of intuitions. For consciousness exists for itself only through what was thought. A stream of intuitions flows constantly into the soul through the senses, causing the "foreignness" of the perceptual picture. Perceptions too are worked out in thinking, becoming past thoughts. A person can no more endure perceptions in their original fullness of spirit than he can bear living, cosmic thinking. The alienation of the original, universal world: that is the soul. For *whom* did it become alien?

If the soul's attention in perceptual surrender to the world were not continually interrupted by the alternation of surrender and self-ness, the act of perceiving would theoretically be perfect cognition. The "interpretation" of perceptions by thinking would be unnecessary. "Pure" perception means, among other things, the art of perceiving independently of the body. The soul's attention, however, is always divided between the world and its own corporeality. The dependency on the body does not consist in the fact that one cognizes by means of sense organs, but in the soul's attachment to corporeality. Human and world interact completely and spiritually by means of the sense organs: there is total communion. It is only the resulting picture that negates what prevails in the perceiving.

That we only partially experience this communion in perceiving is due to the soul, which guards its "boundaries." Because of the soul's need to feel itself, this communion experience is mere effect—effects on the nervous system, on breathing, on metabolism. Cognition won in mirrored consciousness is accompanied by fine alterations of these systems, whereby the life of cognition, its feeling and will-value, is lost. The original forms of imagination, inspiration and intuition turn into abstract representation, egoistic self-feeling and human instinct.

In sensory perceiving, the human being is passive—things themselves evoke their representations. In this passivity, the lasting identity of world and humanity, the identity of *living* cognizing or of *love*, is slept away. At the same time this loss of identity is the sleeping away, the not-becoming-conscious of the true subject's movement. The distorted shadow of what takes place in this movement—which is an imitative one, "mimicking" what it cognizes and thereby bringing it to expression— falls into ordinary, seemingly passive consciousness. In fact, this imitation is the negative work of the ego or everyday soul, the filtering process which breaks apart total cognition.

In higher cognition, the human keeps himself active and awake. This activity consists in warding off the mediation, the intervention, of the soul. This standing-in-between causes cognizing to fragment into sensations—in which ego consciousness is "passive"—and into conceptuality, whose "production" appears as the activity of this same ego consciousness. The sense world is brought into being through this same "activity," the ego's self-preserving gesture which—because it is unconscious—is interpreted as passivity.

In the imagination the movement itself, which is ordinarily preconscious in the formation of sense pictures, becomes conscious. As a result the "objective" character of the pictures, their numinous givenness, disappears. Consciousness becomes "active" in the realization of self-created pictures; it follows the movement of living thinking. Therefore these pictures are "alive." The cognizer no longer unambiguously stands over against. It is ego consciousness, ruled by the results of unconscious activity, that ordinarily stands apart. In physical sense perception, the human learns of separateness, of the passive use of the sense organs and of the active use of thinking. He is passive in perception, for here the true I plays the main role, but he is active in thinking, for here the main role falls to the ego.

Cosmic living thinking, the *sense* of the "big world," surges through the senses. If a person were capable of receiving this revelation, he would not have to *think* what the sense organs were transmitting.

Sense organs are instruments for the capacity to mediate cognitions without conscious, thinking activity. For themselves, the senses yield "sense" immediately. What thinking then yields is necessary for the soul. Unmediated cognition in this sense is equal to living thinking. If this is re-established in connection with sense perception, we have "pure perceiving."

The path of modern training consists in liberating this movement of the soul from the compulsion of the egocentrically binding experience of the self. It can do so only if it never abandons the principle of cognition. Therefore, training begins with thinking, which is the basis for every judgment: every choice goes through thinking. What is done with thinking becomes the model for the transformation of all the other capabilities of the soul.

In everyday life, will, representation and feelings appear only in relation to an object. Modern training seeks to develop these capabilities in such a way that they can exist without an object. Put another way: these capabilities are withdrawn from their objects. This is only possible if, at the same time, an I is active that does not have to experience itself as a subject in relation to objects. The interdependence of the objectivity of the world and the subjectivity of the cognizer is overcome. At the starting point of the exercise the object is the occasion and guiding principle so that *movement* appears and can be experienced, so that object and activity are experienced as one — always one.

One may realize, theoretically, that cognition belongs to the world as a whole and does not occur outside the events of the world. In experiencing the spiritual identity of the seen with seeing, and of the already thought with thinking, this theoretical result becomes a living experience. Cognizing is the basic component of the world — cognizing is the world. The world is cognizing. The question whether the world changes with cognizing becomes meaningless: cognizing is the world process. Cognizing and the cognizer belong to the world. According to Goethe, both together constitute higher nature.

In experiencing pure thinking, the Living Ideal is clothed in a picture; it becomes a living idea-picture. In pure perceiving, devoid of thought, the idea-element moves into the perceptual picture, where it was originally: perceiving becomes a timeless process. In imagination the picture garment, free of perceptions, receives an ideal content and becomes living archetype.

Things stand completely finished and unmoving before consciousness. They appear to "be" independent of cognition. However, it is consciousness itself that gives things being, for the world is not only manifoldness, but also connectedness. And the world appears in man: the human soul is the stage where not only connections, but also things, appear. Now, consciousness can awaken; it can be trained to become aware of appearance. The beholding of unconnected things, the appearance of connections, the interconnected picture — each is a deed of the spirit in the soul, and the spirit can include its own deed, which is also a world deed, in the picture. Consciousness can see seeing; thus it can become independent of what has been seen and can realize that seeing and the seen are one, can become one. The seen is the result of seeing. It becomes seen in the interruption of seeing and is maintained continuously by seeing—through the superconscious intuition, in which we live constantly and whose death we experience in consciousness. That intuition is true seeing, that is true life.

Consciousness can reach the point where its birth as consciousness and the givenness of being coincide. It can reach the original unity out of which consciousness and being were broken.

This point is superconsciousness, heaven, the heavens. The being of things consists in their having been thought, having been seen, being seen thus, being thus, perceived by consciousness point for point in constant loss and forgetting. For the superconscious there is not a thing and, separate from it, its thought or its being seen; for the superconscious no "thing" exists—no half-thought, no interrupted thinking, no forgetting of thinking.

To forget thinking, cognizing, to forget what we do, is a sin: in Christianity, Peter's sin.

Peter's sin—forgetting what one is doing—is the seed of Judas' sin: betrayal. In traditional cultures, it was not necessary to develop a consciousness of one's own activity. The identity of self and world was still unbroken. Only with the appearance of modern consciousness was the problem of autonomy posed. The beginnings of total autonomy are realized in physical-mathematical thought, in self-alienation and in identification with the physical object. Modern thinking throws light on everything—but provides no light for the producer of this light! The root of its activity is immersed in a supersensible world-reality. If this step to its own actual sources does not occur, an antagonistic power works itself out in consciousness, which in this regard is unfree. It forces us merely to apply thinking. Mere "application" of thinking engenders betrayal: thinking denies its spiritual essence. It traces itself back to something extraspiritual which, again, can only be recognized through thinking. Theoretical denial becomes practical fact. The materialistic world picture and the praxis which derives from it are the result of that forgetting, culminating inexorably in this betrayal. We take the mirrored picture seriously, and do not notice the process of reflection. Thus the mirrored world wins its apparent self-sufficiency. At the same time, the way is paved for man's abdication from the source of his freedom.

If forgetting is suspended, the foreignness, the otherness of the perceived world disappears: it reveals its essence to intuition, i.e., to spiritual observation in thinking. In meditation, for example, we proceed from a symbol or theme, until the inner movement with which we think the theme becomes identical with the theme itself. We simultaneously experience this identity as spiritual experience itself. Intensively understood, all meditative efforts of perception (*Wahr-nehmen*) submerge themselves in the essence of truth (*Wahr-heit*). Truth as presence, unconcealedness, unforgetting, unlostness: "Aletheia."

Pure perceiving can only be realized by one who is capable of remaining awake without thinking thoughts: one who has experienced that his own being is not what seems to be his property, who has experienced that the world does not realize itself outside cognition, but *in* it, in phases which, at first, lie above human consciousness. Cognition, experienced as world process, looks upon

one reality, in whose formation human beings participate. Mirrored cognition and the world beheld in it have
broken apart out of unity. This is why seeing and light,
thinking and world, fit so well together. "They must
have been meant for each other." Music, every color,
every word turn inward without relinquishing themselves, into the center of the wakeful silence.

The Spiritual Communion of Modern Humanity

Perceiving precedes thinking.
Perceiving precedes perception.
Perception precedes consciousness.

Thinking precedes what has been thought.
What has been thought precedes consciousness.
Consciousness is kindled by what has been thought.
Consciousness is not kindled by what has been perceived.

Perception is already there without a perceiver.
Perception becomes conscious, is always there for awareness; but awareness is still not consciousness.

Consciousness arises through thinking. Thinking arises in what has been perceived, and reflects upon it. It reflects upon itself, turned away from perception. Thus consciousness arises through thinking, in what has been thought.
Consciousness does not experience what precedes it: i.e., thinking, perceiving. It arises from what has been thought; it contains what has been perceived.

First, the perceiving is there, then what has been perceived; then thinking about what has been perceived; then thinking about itself; then what has been thought and consciousness.

Awareness is dull, dreaming consciousness. Only perceptions are there.

Thinking is still contained in perceiving. Perceiving is still a thinking of the senses.

Awareness does not know about itself, only about the perceived. Therefore it is not consciousness.

The perceived still contains what has been thought. Therefore both are alive.

The child who does not yet say "I" is not yet corporeality. He perceives this just as he does anything else. The true I, which still speaks out of him, does not see itself. The subject is always invisible. The true I still submerges itself in the world, as it does in the child's body. It experiences the world as its own corporeality; everything is third person for the I.

This experience, the submerging, is boundless.

Ancient peoples looked at the world in this way. They were in knowledge without being knowers.

Clarity comes from what has been thought. What was perceived was clear, while the consciousness was dull.

Thinking precedes consciousness and is preceded by perceiving.

What precedes thought can become neither the content nor the object of consciousness.

Consciousness is asleep in thinking and in perceiving.
Consciousness is awake in what has been thought, what has been perceived.
What has been thought and what has been perceived are the boundaries of consciousness. Without these boundaries, consciousness falls asleep.

There is no empty consciousness.
Consciousness guards its boundaries.
The boundaries form consciousness.
The boundaries are consciousness.
The boundaries guard consciousness.
Consciousness does not behold thinking.
Consciousness does not see perceiving.

Thinking cannot be explained. Why is logic logical? Why is evidence evident? If it could be explained at all, it could only be explained by new, evident thinking.

Perceiving cannot be explained. Why is this blue, that red? If it could be explained at all, it could only be explained by a new perceiving.

Thinking mediates the world. Perceiving mediates the world—through what has been thought, through what has been perceived.

Thinking itself is immediate cognition.
Perception itself is immediate cognition.
The world is immediate cognition.
The human being sleeps in immediate cognition.
Consciousness awakes in mediation.

The human being needs mediation. He stands in between.

The world is not the world that humanity sees.
The I is not the I that humanity thinks.

Humanity's I is the I that has been thought: a memory of the thoughts of the true I.

The human world is the perceived world, the dead picture of the picture of the world.

Over against the I is the world; over against the world is the I. The boundaries of the I are the boundaries of the world. The boundaries are what consciousness cannot think through, what the eye cannot see through.

The child's I has identified itself with corporeality.

The child now says "I" to corporeality.

The I mirrors itself in corporeality and says "I" — to the mirror image.

Corporeality divides the I from the world.

The mirror turns back the rays of the I.

Corporeality divides the world from the I.

The mirror turns back the rays of the world.

Corporeality divides perceiving from thinking.

The I finds the world in what has been perceived, finds the I in thinking.

The I is the I of consciousness.

The I lives by grace of thinking.

The I lives by grace of perceiving.

The I supports itself on what has been thought, on what has been perceived.

The I supports itself on the world which it sees.

Consciousness becomes clear through what has been thought.

What has been thought is transparent.

The world is darkened when what has been perceived is stripped of thought.

What has been perceived is not transparent.

The world was once the illumined world. The world was open to human beings. Once, human beings did not cognize themselves. They were part of the illumined world.

The light of the world shone through the human being. Being was cognition. Cognition was being.

A human being cognizes the thoughts of another.

He assimilates the thoughts of others into his thinking. In thinking, what has been thought receives new life. A human being sleeps in thinking, sleeps in what is alive.

He thinks the thoughts of the other as if they were the product of his own thinking. Otherwise there would be no understanding.

In thinking the thoughts of another, a human being extinguishes himself. He becomes identical with the other's thinking. He falls asleep. He is the other. He is the other's thinking.

The human being thinks his thoughts. He sleeps while thinking. He awakens in what has been thought. He extinguishes himself in thinking. He is thinking.

The human being is able to submerge in the other. But during the submerging he is asleep, like the child who is not yet in the body. Awareness is there, without consciousness: understanding without the one who understands.

Where is thinking? Where is the I? Where is the where?
Every where comes from thinking. Thinking is no-where.

Thinking is everywhere. But not what has been thought.

It is the I that has boundaries. The I is boundary itself.
The I is what has been thought, what has been perceived:
the remembered, the past, the mirror image.

The I is the true I. It is not body, not soul, not spirit. It
is the I, it is spirit, it is understanding. It is everywhere. It
is asleep everywhere. It mirrors itself on the body. It has
no boundaries. It is boundlessness. It is boundless understanding, submerged into the other, into otherness. The I
precedes consciousness.

Humanity cognizes the world. The world is the other.
The human being perceives the other. The other is what
has been perceived. Perceiving precedes what has been
perceived.

In perceiving, the human being is asleep. In perceiving,
the human being forgets himself. The more he forgets
himself, the better he perceives. In perceiving, the human
being extinguishes himself.

Nevertheless the human being is present in perceiving;
otherwise, who would perceive?

In hearing music a human being does not think. One
forgets oneself in music. The more one forgets oneself,
the better one hears the music. It is not the tones one
hears, but the music.

The tones are where the music is not. Music is streaming, like rays, warmth, life.

Words are not thinking. Words are where thinking is not.

Thinking is streaming, as are rays, warmth, music. Words exist in order to guide the streaming, like stones in a brook.

Things are not the world. Things are what one sees. Things are letters, words. Where the world is not, things are. The world is thinking, the world is music, the world is streaming life, the world wants to be read: the world wants to be played like music.

Otherwise it remains letter, note, stone.

In perceiving, the human being goes out. He extinguishes himself, becomes the other.

Humanity has the capability of submerging in the other. Where is the I?

Sleeping, the I enters the other. The other is no longer the other; it is the place of the I.

The I is in the world. The I is identical with the world. The body too is world.

Humanity is in the world. Humanity is part of the world.

Reading is supersensible. Reading is not copying. Reading is bringing to life once more.

The human being does not read letters, words, or thoughts. The human being can read the living meaning.

One can read texts; one can read musical notes.

One can read things of the world.

The human being reads the world. Every act of cognition is reading, even the most elementary cognition is a spelling-out.

The cognized world is the illumined world. The human being cognizes the world.

The human being cognizes himself: he is part of the illumined world.

Out of the human being, the light of the world illuminates the world.

The human being became the dwelling place of the light.

Being is cognition. Cognition is being.

The otherness of the world is of the same sort as the foreignness of the other's thoughts.

The otherness of the world is of the same sort as the foreignness of all contents of my intuition.

For the ego, the whole world of the true I is foreign.

For the ego, the otherness of the world is the boundary.

The ego is the otherness of the world.

But the world is the I.

The ego sees the seen world.

In seeing, the ego extinguishes itself.

In seeing, the ego sleeps.

In seeing, the I wakes. It keeps watch over the sleep of the ego.

The ego sleeps; this is the wakefulness of the I.

The dream is what is foreign. What has been seen is foreign for the ego.

Without foreignness the ego would not be. The other exists for the sake of the ego. The other guards the ego.

The I beholds the landscape, the sky, the tree.

The ego extinguishes itself. The landscape, the sky, the tree are places of the I. Landscape, sky, tree are: I.

The I does not know about itself. The I does not know about landscape, sky, tree. The I is landscape, sky, tree.

The I sees nothing.

The ego sees landscape, sky, tree. It knows about landscape, sky, tree.

It knows about itself.

The ego experiences the world and itself.

The ego is there to become experience.

Experience is there so that experiencing might become experience.

Not for the ego.

The ego arises after experiencing.

The ego arises in experience.

For the ego, thinking cannot become experience, only what has been thought.

For the ego, perceiving cannot become experience; only what has been perceived can become experience.

The human being is what is remembered, the human being is the past. Consciousness forms itself on dead things.

The human being is individuality in the realm of the dead.

Thinking is life.

Perceiving is life.

The ego extinguishes itself in life.

The human being sleeps in life.

The human being lives the sleep of life.

In the death of life, the human being awakens.

Death is never experience. *That* it is never experienced is death.

The experience of death is resurrection. Life.

Death is there to become experience.

Thinking is the continual dying of thinking.

Thinking itself is life.

Perceiving is the continual dying of perceiving.

Perceiving itself is life.

Thinking is there to be experienced.

Perceiving is there to be experienced.

In experiencing, the subject awakens, not the ego.

The true subject needs no boundaries. It does not need what has been thought, what has been perceived. It does not need the other.

The true subject does not think, does not feel, does not will. It is. I am.

Humanity does not know who it is.

It must will this knowing.

Nothing draws humanity onward. It has become the thinker.

And all statements stem from thinking.

From now on there is no "teaching" for human beings.

A person must will it.

A person cannot will thinking, only what has been thought.

In his thinking, a person can will what has been thought, concentratedly, purely, for itself. A pure idea.

A person can concentrate on a pure idea.

The pure idea is transparent, shadowless. It does not exist, cannot be remembered. When a person does not will it, it does not exist. It lives out of the will of the person who beholds the pure idea. Through the pure idea a person beholds thinking. In the pure idea. Not what has been thought. The idea has no past. It lives out of the living will of the human being.

If a human being is clear, he beholds living thinking.

The idea no longer needs to be thought. It is already thought. It only wishes to be beheld.

Whoever beholds living thinking is the true subject.

Living thinking is will and feeling.

The true subject beholds the living.

The true subject sees the death of life.

It is the true subject.

Life is light. Not biology.

The true subject does not stand over against living thinking. It is not an object. It is identical with living thinking. As with landscape, sky, tree.

The light shines through the I, this world, life, thinking, perceiving.

The ego sacrifices itself for the I. It is the I.

The dead sacrifices itself for life. The light shines through death: life.

Thinking was withdrawn from the dead, from the object. The human being does not tie himself to the finished, to the past. He is present in thinking, present to it. Now the present is achieved. Usually one sleeps through it and awakens in the past. Only the past has future. The present is continual presence. Continual: that means not in time. For time is continual death. But the present lives.

Whoever beholds thinking, lives. Whoever lives, needs no boundaries.

Whoever needs no boundaries can surrender himself. To the world, to another. To living thinking.

Everything is made from living thinking. Whoever surrenders himself to living thinking, cognizes. He cognizes everything as himself, as his I, as an I. Surrender is love. Only the I-am can love.

Only the unafraid can love. Fear requires boundaries.

To be an individual without boundaries means to be alive, means to be an individual in what is alive, not in what is dead.

Only something dead can be property; only something dead needs property. Thought belongs to me, but not thinking.

The true I has nothing. It is everything. Only he can possess who is not everything.

Living thinking belongs to the world. Does it belong to the I? It is the world. It is the I.

The beholding of the spirit is immediacy, unmediated cognition. To illuminate the mediating and the mediation at the same time is art. Cognizing is as natural as any art.

Art is always there; it only has obstacles.

Obstacles for art are fingers, strings, notes. They must all become transparent—cleared away, just as the eye is not there in seeing. Mediation is the obstacle, the ripples through which transparent being becomes opaque.

If the obstacles are eliminated, art is there. It is always there.

I am the greatest obstacle. When the I is extinguished, the I is there. The world is there in its illuminedness.

Illuminedness is the primal characteristic of the world. Opacity comes from man, so that the light might shine.

The hand must begin to become hand-at-the-keyboard. Everything learned, everything practiced, is forgotten. The hand is led back to its origin.

Thinking is led back from what has been thought to the source. The source does not lie before us. The source is in us. The source is always there.

Whenever there is no obstacle, it lights up.

Light knows of no standstill.

The spirit is continual understanding. There is nothing

at all that is understood. There is nothing at all that could be understood.

The picture of the world is the picture of the human being. There is no picture of the world that is not seen by humanity.

The world is always the seen world. The unseen picture is not seen by anyone, only thought up.

The picture is already the result of beholding. Before beholding there is oneness. Without the beholder, there is no picture, only opaque oneness.

The human being is in the picture. He releases himself from the picture and becomes the beholder. The picture changes.

When you speak, it is you. When you are silent, it is you.

How could you be you without being you?

In beholding, the human being sleeps. He awakens in the beheld. The beheld has already been thought.

The beheld is the objective world for human beings.

The true I is never separated from the world. It is in the immediate cognition.

The ego is separation. For the ego, the world is not illumined.

The true light shines in the world and in human beings. It is a single light.

Where the boundary is, light is reflected—by the darkness. The mirrored light lights up the world. The illumined world becomes objective for us.

The unified light is divided. Physical light remains outside; inside, the light of thought arises.

Humanity withdraws from the world. What is left behind is spatiality, space.

Humanity withdraws from the present. What remains is time, the past. These we leave behind.

Our withdrawal changes the picture. We behold the changed picture. That is our objective world.

For humanity, the beheld world is the alien deity.

Humanity is not present in the beholding. The dream picture becomes alien to it, divine, objective and uncognizable.

The beheld world is a patchwork. We search for the connection. The more connections we find, the more pieces remain. The true connection is not between the pieces. The patchwork is what fell out of the connection.

First there is music. Then rhythm, then notes.

First there is meaning. Then thoughts, then sentences, then words, then letters. But there are also relationships between letters.

Through perceiving and thinking, measuring takes place. The measured itself is perception.

The fragment is dead. The connection between the fragments also.

Humanity creates the picture of the world: the perceived.

Humanity creates thoughts: what has been thought.

Spelling-out connects what has been perceived with what has been thought. A first reading.

The idea can be beheld—not what has been thought. Idea is picture.

Picture is idea. Every sensible experience is already theory.

Thinking is directed back to the metaphoric reference, not the the perceived picture.

Perceiving is directed back to the beholding of the idea,

not to what has been thought.

Living thinking is idea-forming.*

Living perceiving is picture-idea-beholding.

Perceiving and thinking were once immediate cognizing.

In immediacy, the human being is identical with the world.

He is not identical. He is the world.

Identity is always there. Boundaries are for the ego.

The ego becomes experience for the I. The I is the world.

Identity is always there. Otherwise there would be no cognizing. Not even in the patchwork.

We forget our thinking, we forget our perceiving. We deny our thinking through thinking, we deny perceiving through perceiving.

At the same time, we take what has been perceived to be objective, because our thinking is subjective.

We must slow down our life. We do everything too fast.

There is the tree.

I see: there is the tree.

I think that I see: there is the tree.

I think: there is the tree.

There is the tree.

To behold without thoughts is not to behold without thinking.

To truly perceive means to shine simultaneously through the perceived, the perceiving and the perceiver.

---

*The German word here is *bilden*, which means *to form*. It serves as a play on words, since the next sentence refers to *Bild*, which means *picture*. In German, the two words are related, one can say: *Ich bilde das Bild*. I form the picture. — Trans.

Then the complete picture arises.

Thinking belongs to the world. Humanity belongs to the world.

Perceiving belongs to the world. Cognizing belongs to the world.

Nothing is outside. Art belongs to the world. True cognizing is art.

As natural as any art.

The opacity is there so that the light might shine.
The light shines so that we might behold the light.
At first we see what is illumined, not the light.
Art is seeing the source of light at the same time.
Art is seeing the seer at the same time.
That is the transformation.
First we must notice that we are asleep in our thinking.
First we must notice that we are asleep in our perceiving. First we must wake up. Not through what has been thought but in thinking.

First we must wake up. Not through what has been perceived, but in perceiving.

Otherwise the image becomes for us the alien deity, before whom we kneel.

The illuminated world, the hard world, the external deity, thrusts us back onto ourselves.

Through hardness we learn to be feeling beings. We learn to be experiencers. We learn that we are the other.

The hard mineral is our first boundary.

The hard boundary teaches us to be the experiencer beyond the boundaries. Every boundary points beyond itself.

One who is without boundaries is harder than a diamond.

The hardness is not immediacy, it only seems to be.

Immediacy is unbounded life.

Hardness is the result of the immediacy that at first we sleep through.

If we sleep through it, we know only of the world's hardness.

The world's hardness educates towards love: to ever-greater love. Love is nothing natural. Love needs opacity in order to shine through it. Love needs hardness in order to glow through it. Only a human being can love. Angels do not love; they are already everything. Nothing remains for them to love.

Only the other can be loved. Otherness is there so that love might appear.

If love is there, otherness is no more.

The eyes seal the identity and see the other.

The eyes recall identity in that they see the other. In seeing, the eye is illumined. The light illuminates the other. I am the other, shone through. Love transforms the world.

Cognizing is not eating, but reading.

Cognizing is metamorphosed identity.

Identity is metamorphosed cognizing.

Humanity eats the bread. Thus it becomes human and the bread becomes bread. The transubstantiation is accomplished.

The Sense of Being

AWARENESS is not yet consciousness, because it does not yet know anything about itself.

A dull awareness of the world is still an active identity with the world, but without the consciousness of it. For that consciousness to arise, it had to be cut out of the world, thereby breaking the identity.

Unconsciously and in diminished form, the original identity lives on, even today, in each act of cognition.

The dullness, too, is present today, in another form. We forget thinking, forget perceiving, because we are only awake in what has been thought, in to what has been perceived.

We constantly appeal to thinking, to perceiving, even when denying them by thinking and perceiving. We know that we become aware of everything through them, but we attribute reality only to what has been thought and to what has been perceived, not to perceiving and to thinking.

How do we recognize something as having reality? By perceiving and thinking, a thinking which, however, we declare to be unreal—an ego game that could not take place without the possibility of the true I's immanence in thinking and perceiving.

In our perceiving, we try to return to a unity with the world.

The more we forget ourselves in beholding, the better we see.

Is pure perceiving the same as the original dull awareness of the world?

Pure perceiving is willed. Pure perceiving encounters obstacles, and, in overcoming these obstacles, pure perceiving arises. Without these obstacles there would be no willing, no overcoming, no one who could will — no pure perceiving. The obstacles awaken pure perceiving.

Every mediation is an obstacle. Mediation is there to be sublated. The sublation is a transillumination. All art consists in mediating and at the same time transilluminating the mediation.

The mediation is there to be done away with.

Corporeality is an obstacle to seeing. But without it, there would be no seer.

In pure thinking and in pure perceiving, mediation sees through itself. Therefore pure thinking and perceiving are artistic activities. Cognizing is the essential art.

Truth is true-ness, *aletheia: a-letheia*, not-forgetting, not-extinguishing. It is the consciousness that does not extinguish itself in cognizing, from which nothing remains unconcealed in the act of cognition. Even the act of cognition is unconcealed.

Truth is absolute unconcealment.

Unconcealment is original light. Unreflected, it penetrates the perceived, perceiving and perceiver at the same time.

Pure perceiving is presence, like the experience of living thinking.

Presence is pure presentness, in time and space, un-pastness. It knows no time.

Because it knows no time, it knows no thoughts, no perceptions.

And yet it is fully concentrated. On what? It is an aiming without a target. A fulfilled being-empty, a being-there (*Dasein*). Nothing else.

We learn slowly to remain awake in the present. Without supporting ourselves on the past, without resting on the memory of ourselves, we learn to be present, to be there. Not over against the world, but in the world, where we always are. What time is for the past, space is for the over-against, the opposed. Both are the loss of the world. Loss of presentness. Loss itself: forgetting, becoming concealed. The opposite of truth.

To learn to be empty and, at the same time, to be ready is art. The emptiness never becomes full, and the readiness never changes into something else. They endure.

Nothing is more fulfilled than readiness. It contains all possibility. It is freedom, flashing from moment to moment and everlastingly from freedom to freedom.

What has been thought is there to be re-thought.

Re-thought, what has been thought becomes living, only to die again immediately.

Thoughts are raised from the dead where words are

not. Signs are there to direct the stream of life to where words are not.

Meaning is between the words, between the signs, between the sentences. The resurrection of what has been thought is reading.

Where resurrection does not occur, there is no reading, no thinking, but copying (*Abbilden*). There is rhetoric.

Rhetoric is the external connection of signs. The signs do not dissolve and do not point beyond themselves. Reading itself is the overcoming of signs. Higher reading is the overcoming of reading. Mediation is done away with, step by step.

Only a few can truly read a text. There is hardly anyone left who can read the perceptual image. Even the claim that perceptions can only be read is forgotten.

Facts, objective reality independent of the perceiver, independent of the reader—though he read ever so primitively—these are the uncognized, unillumined mediations of which we know nothing. We only know the cognized, cognizing's product. Cognizing itself remains uncognized for us.

The numinosity of the deity without rests on its appearing independent of the human being.

The objective material world is numinous because its act of appearing has been slept through.

Appearance is the act of appearing slept through.

We sleep through the ever-enduring identity because it endures on a level which our ordinary consciousness cannot penetrate. Only the dream appears to us, adamantine, like a deity. A numen.

We know nothing of our identity with this deity.

Pre-Christian humanity knew nothing of its identity with the world, but for another reason: there was as yet no one who could have known about the identity. The human was still identical: undivided, unborn.

The human being today knows about himself, even when he denies and disowns both himself and this knowledge. He knows nothing of his identity with the world, because he owes his consciousness to the destruction of it.

By not illuminating the mediation, by not looking through it, he worships a false deity.

The deity of ancient humanity was still spirit, therefore true deity. The deity of modern humanity, whose numinosity it does not recognize, is erected by humanity itself: it is an idol. We give it life—our own. We lend it spirit—our own. But we do not notice this.

This idolatry of objective reality is the first step.

Worship of evil follows.

The idol of modern humanity seems to be morally neutral. But a glance at its effects teaches otherwise: the human being is dehumanized by this religion. He himself becomes what he cognizes as the world.

First he considers himself to be matter, then this belief works miracles: he immediately ceases to be human.

When he realizes that his world can bring him nothing good, that his world, the way he sees it, holds nothing but ruin upon ruin, then he will bow his head before a deity which he knows is evil. Every human being helps this along. Everyone builds on the technological world, producing or consuming. One cannot do otherwise.

But we know from experience that this world of technology will bring nothing good to us. By living in this world, we affirm it, and if we fail to transilluminate it in our affirmation, if we fail to recognize what it truly is, hence if we fail to practice the art of cognizing, then we affirm its evil idol too.

The whole world awaits this gesture, even the world of technology.

The redeeming of the world lies in cognizing it in truth.

All cognizing is magic. Incomplete cognizing bewitches. The world is always the cognized world.

The world picture is made by human beings. There is no other picture of the world.

But we ourselves belong to the world. Therefore our cognizing belongs to the world, too. The world picture is incomplete and distorted when an element that belongs to the picture does not appear in it.

Today we cognize as if we were standing outside the world picture; we think it is there without us, without our cognizing, that we look upon something that is finished.

On the other hand, we think that we belong completely to the cognized world, and are like it. But this cognized world contains nothing that would be capable of cognition, nothing that could cognize.

The word belongs to the world, so do concept, idea and thought—even if we live in the illusion that the world is there, finished, without conceptuality.

Once the world of ideas, spirituality, was a reality for human beings. The idea-less sensible world was mere appearance for them. Today, the idea-less sensible world is reality. Ideality is at best for us the product of the non-ideal, a will-o'-the-wisp.

We recognize the non-ideal as non-ideal through ideas. But is not the non-ideal after all an idea?

Nothing else is cognizable for us except conceptuality, ideality.

Matter too is an idea.

Conceptuality has died in us, has become a thing of the past. This is why it seems so vaporous, so airy.

Present human consciousness is a consciousness of the past. No life penetrates it.

But one who is not past can behold what is past, what is dead. However, we can forget this beholding that we always practice. Then we sell our freedom for a mess of pottage, for sense-based reality, which the ancients still recognized as a world of appearance. Dead conceptuality within stands over against solid, hard outer reality, the world of objects, that is to say, the world of dead objects, which are calculably moved by external, subjectless but calculable forces—the world of physics.

In standing over against the object, humanity could cognize itself as the one-who-stands-over-against. It could behold the condition of standing-over-against in itself, and in this beholding pass over into freedom. But humanity can also forget the experience in the experience, and sell its freedom, stepping—as an object—into the world of calculability.

In the old dull consciousness, in awareness, both thinking and perceiving were still alive and united.

United, therefore alive. Alive, therefore binding humanity. Freedom was not possible.

The world picture of dull awareness changed into the

world of objects, into the world of facts, which stands over against. Humanity fell out of the world. It fell out of eternity, out of true space. Therefore time arises, abstract space and the world standing over against us.

Out of the living world picture, out of the world that was the illumined world of living cognition, life moved into the perceptual picture, understanding moved into the human thought-world. Dead thinking, however, cannot cognize life in the perceptual world. It senses life out there, and is always searching for it. It worships this un-cognized, never-attained life — as the objective world of matter.

Objects are metamorphosed spirit. Thoughts are meta-morphosed spirit. Metamorphosis is there to allow for freedom.

Nevertheless freedom remains only a possibility so long as object and thought do not become a living unity again in humanity. But there is no permanent possibility. Every possibility passes.

The older a possibility grows, the more difficult it is to realize. The more it passes, the more difficult it is to find again. An art can be lost.

Life in the spirit, pure perceiving, is like music.

The musician breaks the spell paralyzing the notes, the instrument, his hand, his breath.

He reads and breaks the spell by uniting the functions of his body and those of the instrument in a union that can be neither prescribed nor analyzed.

The hearing of music belongs to the making of music. Producing and hearing interpenetrate each other. Hearing is already producing, in that it simultaneously perceives and regulates the producing. Producing and cognizing act at the same time and as one. They are one and the same activity.

The musical creation then makes its way to the "passive" hearer. If he is musical, i.e., can read, music reaches him. But if he cannot read, or reads imperfectly, then he turns the music into tone, acoustics and harmony. If he is an unmusical person, only noise reaches him. Only vibrations reach the scientist who suppresses or pushes aside his musicality. For him, even tone is already something read. His basic principle, however, is not to read. Therefore he does not notice that the vibrations, which he attributes to the tone, must also be read in order to exist at all. Every perception, by means of which he proves his vibrations, always already contains the element by means of which he will explain his perceptions, and these are much more complex than the vibrations themselves. He is playing possum with himself. He acts as though he could not read—until he really does forget how.

What was created as music does not change in the space that receives and transmits it. It only changes through us: by our not-understanding. What seems to vibrate in space, without a conductor, is music—always music. In the music that lives in hearing, what should inaudibly change?

Hearing music is not like hearing words.

Words are read along with thoughts. Thoughts are in some cases read along with meaning that transcends thought.

Music is not elevated to meaning by means of thoughts or by means of thinking. Music is not interpreted like a perception. It is only heard.

In hearing, one does not interpret; there is no standing-over-against. It is not we who are present, only the music: we are it. What transcends thought is heard; true hearing is sublime understanding, pure perceiving.

What one cannot fully read becomes signs, letters, notes, tones. Behind these, total reality is concealed. But for the nonreader the signs themselves are a reality, whereas for one who learns to read they are seeds that germinate within him. From the hard kernels, he can slowly release sleeping life from its spell.

Hearing does not happen with the ear. For a "non-hearing" ear the singer sings in vain.

Hearing does not occur in time. In music, sequence amounts to nothing. What has gone before is always present, along with what is yet to come; otherwise it is not music. The further back and forward my present extends, the better musician I am.

Hearing naturally takes place in time. Through hearing, time is also suspended.

Art and realism are opposites. Naive realism is only possible when perceiving becomes utterly inartistic. Any "objective" realism is naive. Any contrasting of being and cognizing, of life and knowledge, is realism, is a lie: through cognizing, I assert being; through cognizing, I deny cognizing.

Objects, facts, things, are there because I cannot read, because I cannot guide them to resurrection, because I do not notice that they are signs—because I am "unmusical."

The body is an obstacle to beholding, but without it there would be no one to behold.

If I could be completely musical in tasting, seeing, smelling, the whole world would dawn for me as living music. There is no past music, as there is no static light; music is always flowing.

Whether music or picture, every art leads to life. Not to the dead picture of life (normally designated as life) but to true life, which is at the same time light.

No mirrored, dead light, but light which simultaneously shines through the cognized and the cognizer.

What is the reality of music? Where is the reality of music?

In man? Outside man?

The reality of the world is the living, superrational sense that awaits enchanted in every sign to be awakened into life.

Understand how true cognizing is an art, a lost art!

Pure perceiving is for the world and for you what musical hearing is for music and for you.

Understand what you are making of the world when you do *not* behold it with pure perceiving!

What is the sense of music?

In the question only the questioning has meaning and sense.

The answer is unnecessary. It lies in making music.

The question is only possible before making music.

The answer is the silencing of the question in making music.

There is no answer aside from music.

Ancient humanity had more sense than we. Breathing, eating, the sex act were for it processes of cognition. The heart, kidney, lungs were organs of cognition for it.

In pure perceiving the whole human being becomes eye, ear, thinking organ.

In the ancient world, the *consciousness* of identity with the cosmos was mystery knowledge. Even today it is so, but from the opposite pole.

What, then, is the sense of Being?

The Light of the Earth

THE EARTH

THE earth is what we see. As we see it, so it is.

Our seeing and the earth cannot be distinguished. If we do not see the earth, we see nothing at all.

The earth exists in our consciousness; everything we perceive, everything we know about, is in our consciousness, including ourselves.

This seeing is not subjective. If it were, we could see whatever we wanted, for example, white as black or yellow. But then there would be no sense in speaking of something as white, black or yellow.

Seeing is objective. It is a whole world process: the world brings about seeing. The world sees itself through human beings.

But, in what we call earth, seeing itself is not contained. The earth is beheld through seeing.

THE HEAVENS

Cognizing is not of this world, not of the earth; through cognizing, the earth becomes this worldly world. Cognizing is a heavenly gift; its home is heaven. Were it earthly, it could not cognize the earth. Thereby the human being is a child of heaven. But in his noncognizing being he is a child of the earth. Insofar as he is truly human, however, he joins heaven and earth through his soul. When one speaks of higher forms of cognition, one means heavens: first, second and third heaven.

In that we see the earth, we are heaven. Were we ourselves earth, we could not see the earth. We have a share in the earth, otherwise we would not see the earth. We have a share in heaven, otherwise we would not see at all. If we could not see, we would not be human. We would not be. We are human so long as we see the earth.

THE SEEN

Still, seeing belongs wholly to heaven. Where seeing comes to a standstill, where it no longer penetrates, is earth. Where the light rebounds, is reflected, appears what is seen, the veil.

The veil is not darkness. If it were, it could not be illuminated by the light. Were darkness illuminated, it would cease to be darkness. Darkness is the play of light and darkness: the earth, color. The human being is opacity, also the mix of light and darkness: he is the prism through which the colors are seen, multiplicity. In him the transformation takes place. Hence the earth itself has the nature of light. What is seen is related to light, otherwise it would not be visible. The nature of the earth is to be visible.

But human seeing reaches only to the surface, to the veil. For in human seeing, the light breaks, becomes form and surface, becomes the world: it appears. The world appears—the world which is seen, which is illumined. The light appears against the background of human not-cognizing, in the darkness.

Seeing does not penetrate, a veil arises, because of human beings. We hold fast to the heavenly gift; we do not surrender everything, do not surrender ourselves wholly: we want to sense ourselves in the process. Therefore our seeing reaches only to the boundary. Our seeing is the seen, the boundary of seeing, which of itself would be boundless, as is heaven: pure transparency, the true light.

THE TRUE LIGHT

The true light illumines nothing; it is itself everything. We do not know this light, because we are of it. Pure transparency: this is understanding without an object, without a subject, a pure happening, the Word. On earth a subject and an object are needed so that the verb or predicate may bridge the gap between them—may appear, may shine. The true light lights everything, all human beings, not only so that they might appear and become capable of cognizing everything, even light itself, but so that the light might light them, place them in the light, in being. That human beings are, is their light. That the earth is, is its light. But that the earth is, is also its darkness. And even the darkness is cognized through the light. We see the darkness because we have a share in the light.

THE PRELUDE

Everything that appears at any given stage is a prelude to a higher cognizing, a veil that shows itself to us so that we shall not be blinded by what remains hidden behind it. All things are veils on which our cognitive powers and our I's mature. The task is to behold what the veil conceals.

Everything that appears is a letter, to be grasped by a higher reading released from the forms of the letters, from the veil. The letters, as given forms, are a veil, covering the word. By the reader's renunciation of the forms of the letters, the letters lead to the word.

First is the word, then the letters: its sign.

The whole world is sign language. We do not notice what it is: a tapestry of signs. To be overcome by the world means to accept it as the final reality, as thing-ness (*Dinglichkeit*)—without reading.

Everything that appears is a veil. Everything that does not read in us is body. Where we read, we are sense organs. The whole body could be a sense organ. Every level of cognition needs a body.

THE IMITATING

We perceive by following what we perceive with subtle inner movement. Any outer movement would have an effect, an influence upon us; it would be neither perceiving nor cognizing. Cognizing consists precisely in this: following what is to be cognized with our subtler organisms as we follow another's thought with our thinking. We imitate, and, through our imitating gesture, we cognize. Cognizing is in this inner imitation.

We follow a movement with the eyes, with the sense of movement, with the attention. We follow speech with the inner speech of our whole moving being. We follow music not with an outward gesture, though music tempts us to do that, but with inner movement and balance; we follow song with inner song. The more outer movement is aroused, the less understanding there is.

Imitation has different stages: it is a faculty. Ordinarily we experience the resistance of our own being where imitation stops. In everyday life we cognize by means of this resistance. Imitation of the mimicry of the world or its gestures can become conscious. In the third heaven, we wholly adopt its physiognomy.

TRANSUBSTANTIATION

Imitatio is cognizing imitation. It leads to transformation into the one we see. It is not mimicry; the animal does not know the color it assumes. That is *immutatio naturalis*, whereas in the eye that beholds a color an *immutatio spiritualis* takes place: an "intendedness" — a turning towards. The eye does not take on the color, it sees it; it is affected by the color *per modum intentionis*.

But the human being does not remain untouched by what has been seen. His subtler organism, soul and spirit, with which he imitates, begins to resemble what he cognizes. The more completely he cognizes, the more he becomes the one whom he cognizes. Therefore it is said:

"But we all, with open face beholding as in a glass the glory of the Lord, are changed into the same image from glory to glory, even as by the Spirit of the Lord." (2 Cor. 3:18)

"Beloved, now are we the sons of God, and it doth not yet appear what we shall be: but we know that, when he shall appear, we shall be like him; for we shall see him as he is." (1 John 3:2)

In Dante's *Paradiso* it is the degree of seeing which determines the stage of being and the hierarchical level of the angelic beings and blessed human beings. Giving himself up to beholding the eternal light-source through which the world is sustained and illumined in its existence, Dante is penetrated and moved by the same cosmic power that maintains the sun and the stars in motion in their orbits: First Love.

IDENTITY

Cognizing, imitation, always occurs from above. Cognizing is only possible because a more perfect cognition (and imitation) exists behind all the veils. Beyond all the levels of cognition there is identity — as the highest unity of cognizer, cognizing and cognized. The realization of this unity and the simultaneous knowledge of it are The Way.

The Way is the bringing about of complete seeing. Not human seeing! Yet if a human being thinks that there is any kind of seeing other than the human, then his seeing is a dream cognized, and he has forgotten that he has only represented it according to his own manner.

Seeing is God's seeing, the world's seeing. God beholds himself; the world beholds itself through us; this seeing has created us and re-creates us daily. Individual essences by virtue of the darkness in us, we fall out of this *single* vision. We live out of this undivided light; we take part in it insofar as we see, insofar as we are human. Therefore it is said:

"For now we see through a glass, darkly; but then face to face: now I know in part; but then shall I know even as also I am known." (1 Cor. 13:12)

"And if any man think that he knoweth any thing, he

knoweth nothing yet as he ought to know. But if any man love God, the same is known of him." (1 Cor. 8: 2–3)

THE SEEN

The seen is not the cause of seeing, but the result of seeing. The great forgetting has hidden this. We think that what we see is already there before we see it. But someone has already seen it, or else we would know nothing about it. First we (or someone else) must see the stone; then we say that the stone is the cause of our seeing it.

The First Seeing is always forgotten. We must have already seen the stone, otherwise we could not determine anything about it; we would not even know that it was there. But then we also could not claim that the stone caused us to see it. For the stone and our seeing are a single cosmic occurrence: its visibility and our vision.

Every stone has its light. This light is the stone itself. Every being has a cognitive character: the world is Logos-created. The nature of the world is light-nature. The light beholds the First Seeing.

THE FIRST SEEING

First Seeing is not experienced by the human being. We sleep through it. In the second seeing, we awaken. We say: there is the world. By that we mean: here I am. The separation, the disengagement from cognizing identity, has already occurred. Traces of this identity can be discovered. The small child does not say, there is the rose. At most it says rose. Or says nothing, only its eyes shine.

First Seeing is complete imitation, identity: a life in God's bosom, without separation. Perceiving is not yet separated from thinking; both are still cosmic life, cosmic life-of-consciousness. Not individual consciousness, but a single breathing, without one who breathes, without anything to breathe. Life in light-filled aliveness, under the Tree of Life, in First Love, which radiates from God to creation and back, a single ray, without mirroring, without deviation from its original direction. Pure Being.

Between First and Second Seeing is the Fall into Sin. The separated self of man is born, the world shatters, First Light shatters. First Love is lost.

THE SENSES

Originally the human being was wholly sense organ. First Love rayed through us, unimpeded. We were wholly an organism of light. The opacity in humanity developed through the Fall into Sin. The single sense organ disintegrated; the human body became opaque, impervious to First Love. Places that retained something of the cosmic-creative rays are today's sense organs; where there is no sense organ, the rays pass through. There, as formerly, the human being sleeps. But in the sense organs we are awake. Thus the sense organs form us: where they are not, life occurs. The sense organs condition the human structure. At every stage the body is the bearer of the sense organs. Thus there are earthly and also celestial bodies. Without a body the human being would not be a cognizer—at any stage of being, of cognizing.

The bearer of the cognitive organs may become self-serving: then the cognitive organs serve the body. Then the body is as if without senses because that human being feels his body with introverted sense organs. Our feeling becomes self-feeling, something felt rather than something that feels; we feel ourselves, instead of feeling the world. The world: the human body, at every level, not merely the physical body.

THE SPIRITUAL WORLD

The spiritual world does not lie behind sensory manifestations, but *before* the sensory, before the earth. Before the cognized, before the cognized becomes cognized — the spiritual world lies in cognizing itself. What later becomes cognized is still present, not as earth, but as heaven. We always go the whole distance: from highest heaven to earth. Only on earth do we wake up. The earth is our waking consciousness. In sleep, in death, in First Seeing, in First Thinking, in First Love, we withdraw into the heavens, lastingly in death, in First Cognizing for a moment. We seek the earth; it is our ground, where we can find ourselves — first as subject, over against object, then perhaps one day as the one who originally separates subject and object, and can say something about the separation. That one must certainly be exalted above the separation. It must be the exalted one in us. We find it when we can renounce everything that is *ours*: all deeds, all knowledge, all feelings, all relationships to the world, to others, to ourselves — so that the possessor might emerge, pure and naked, not the possession. In addition, we must renounce everything that is not our possession, that we have no relationship to, if we think there is such a thing. The exalted one in us needs no ground, no bearer: it is the foundation. Thus it can stay with seeing, without gravitating to what is seen. Thus it can stand still in thinking without striving towards what is thought. It can

stand still in the spirit, in the heavens; it does not fall to
earth. It beholds the earth. And the earth reveals her true
identity to it — that she is the last rung of the celestial lad-
der, the lowest heaven. She is what has fallen from the
upper heavens with humanity, which cannot be separated
from her.

In this Seeing, therefore, the earth truly becomes
heaven once more.

THE LIGHT OF THE WORLD

Now we look at the earth and see her. We look at her and
see her through our cognizing, through the light. But at
first we do not behold and see our cognizing, the light.
Our cognizing and the light are one, as we ourselves are
one with the earth. The light by which we see is the light
of the world. It shines in our darkness; it illumines the
world. The light of the world is the light of the earth.

Slowly the earth begins to become sun; it begins to
shine. The sun in us is our thinking; it can behold itself; it
needs no illumination from outside and cannot have any.

The sun out there belongs to the earth. We have the notion today that the earth belongs to the sun. This will last
only so long as humanity's own sun, its own light, does
not shine in its darkness. The sun was provisionally separated from the earth to create a space for human darkness — provisionally. So that humanity would have space
to send its own light somewhere, and to notice this light,
its own appearance. So that human beings could truly
say: The I am is the light of the world.

Today the light of the world dwells on earth. We see by
means of this light. It surrounds the earth; it is earthly
light. In this earthly light the I am lives.

LIGHT AND BEING

It is not difficult to see that the conceptual, the idea, does not derive from us to be added to sensory things, even though this ideal element makes its appearance in the human being. The idea "copper" is not brought to the copper by us (we do not so much as "invent" the word), but the idea is what makes up the copper. To what would we have brought the word? To copper!

It is the idea that we cognize from the sensory object. The same element which gives the object its qualities — the essence that can be encountered in various forms of appearance — is cognized as a "that." When someone creates a new idea, say, the idea of a dinner fork, the idea exists first; then it must be given outer form, it must be filled with matter. Nature consists of ideas that actualize themselves. The plant, the stone — these do not wait to be actualized by us.

What makes a thing real, what comes to meet us, is always the idea, whether created by man or nature. The means by which a thing is cognized — be it man-made or natural — is its idea. The cognizable is the creative which gives things their being. It is the same as that by which they are cognized.

The creative is living idea. It is the "that" through which something is cognizable, and it is always living. The *universals* are alive. Dead concepts, nominalism, arise only in human beings.

But that makes it possible for us to see universals in their deadness. In this way we may cognize our own aliveness, so that we may thereby behold the aliveness of the universals. Thus are we resurrected. Thus are things resurrected.

THE VICTORY

The worldly world is always the world we behold, the world cognized by everyday consciousness: the earth. It is a sign of humanity's fallen state, but *at the same time* it is a sign of its possible resurrection, which will become out of this hard kernel the resurrection of the earth, of the cosmos.

Only he can overcome the world who has overcome his own "relationships" to the forms of this world. Only he whose consciousness can endure without the forms of the world is free from all clinging to the world; only he can love the world. That means to cognize it in its always unconcealed, true form.

To overcome the world means to behold the world as it was before it became dead in us: to behold it in its aliveness, as heaven. To overcome the world means to behold the earth in the heavens and to bring the heavens to earth. To overcome the world means to look at the earth as it already is in spirit since Golgotha. Since then it has a new light. Since then it is a rising, newly kindled sun.

"These things I have spoken unto you, that in me ye might have peace. In the world ye shall have tribulation; but be of good cheer; I have overcome the world." (John 16:33)

"For whatsoever is born of God overcometh the world: and this is the victory that overcometh the world, even our faith." (1 John 5:4)

To achieve faith and to overcome the world is one and the same victory.

NOTES

Chapter One
THE TWO STAGES OF CONSCIOUSNESS

1. Massimo Scaligero, *La Logica contro l'Uomo* (Rome: Tilopa, 1967), pp. 92, 105ff.
2. Massimo Scaligero, *Trattato del Pensiero Vivente* (Rome: Tilopa, 1961).
3. Rudolf Steiner, *The Philosophy of Freedom*, trans. Michael Wilson (Spring Valley, N.Y.: Anthroposophic Press, 1964), pp. 27, 39, 73.
4. Massimo Scaligero, *Segreti dello Spazio e del Tempo* (Rome: Tilopa, 1963).
5. Rudolf Steiner, *Human and Cosmic Thought* (London: Rudolf Steiner Press, n.d.), p. 61.
6. Rudolf Steiner, *A Road to Self-Knowledge and The Threshold of the Spiritual World*, 3rd ed. (London: Rudolf Steiner Press, 1975).
7. Steiner, *Philosophy of Freedom,* pp. 116–117.
8. Ibid., pp. 118–119.
9. Ibid., p. 217.
10. Massimo Scaligero, *L'Avvento dell'Uomo Interiore* (Florence: Sansoni, 1959), p. 249.
11. Rudolf Steiner, *Theosophy: An Introduction to the Supersensible Knowledge of the World and the Destination of Man* (Spring Valley, N.Y.: Anthroposophic Press, 1971), p. 31.
12. Steiner, *Philosophy of Freedom*, p. 216.

13. Rudolf Steiner, *Das Ewige in der Menschenseele: Unsterblichkeit und Freiheit*, GA 67 (Dornach, Switzerland: Rudolf Steiner Nachlassverwaltung, 1962), Vortrag vom 21.2.1918.

Chapter Three
CONCENTRATION AND CONTEMPLATION

1. Exercises leading to "pure perception" are outlined in Rudolf Steiner's *Knowledge of the Higher Worlds and Its Attainment*, 3rd ed. (New York: Anthroposophic Press, 1947), as well as in other Steiner sources.
2. For the outlined method of exercise, see also: Rudolf Steiner, *Guidance in Esoteric Training*, trans. revised Charles Davy and Owen Barfield (London: Rudolf Steiner Press, 1972), chapter 1; *The Stages of Higher Knowledge*, trans. revised Lisa D. Monges and Floyd McKnight (Spring Valley, N.Y.: Anthroposophic Press, 1967), chapter 1; *An Outline of Occult Science*, trans. Maud and Henry B. Monges, revised Lisa D. Monges (Spring Valley, N.Y.: Anthroposophic Press, 1972), chapter 5. And see: Massimo Scaligero, *La Logica contro l'Uomo,* Part 2, chapter 4; *Yoga Meditazione Magia* (Rome: Teseo, 1971), Parts 10 and 13.

Chapter Four
THE BOUNDARIES OF THE SOUL

1. Steiner, *Theosophy*, chapter 1.
2. Rudolf Steiner, *The Inner Nature of Man and The Life Between Death and a New Birth* (London: Anthroposophical Publishing Co., 1959), pp. 24ff.
3. Scaligero, *Yoga Meditazione Magia*, p. 81.
4. Ibid.

ABOUT THE AUTHOR

Georg Kühlewind was born in 1924 in Central Europe. In a letter destined for this volume, he writes of himself, in English, as follows:

My first interests, at the age of fifteen, were psycho-analysis, Jung, and the history of religions and culture. At seventeen, I became a student of Karl Kerenyi. My tendency was to become a classical philologist in his sense and to learn Latin and Greek. Freud and Jung convinced me that life was not to be understood rationally. I studied economics. I tried to erase all habits, traditions and conventionality in me. I succeeded. There remained only a desert. (At the age of five, I had a very powerful experience of being an I — an experience like Jean Paul's, described by Steiner in *Theosophy.*)

I first met Anthroposophy at the age of eighteen. My feeling was: "That's interesting, but I know it all — it's alive in me." After the War, there came a second meeting: *Truth and Science* and *Goethe's World Conception.* Following this, the cycle of lectures on St. John's Gospel (given in Hamburg) inspired me. I began to read one book after another. And continued to do so for about ten years. Then I felt: this is sterile, I'm not succeeding on the path of inner work (praxis), and this "pile" of knowledge I've been amassing only seems to be a ballast—as indeed it was!

At this point, I nearly threw out the whole of Anthroposophy, but I had a significant dream, and I remembered one of Steiner's books which I knew I had not understood—the *Philosophy of Freedom*. And so I began to study this book and all of Steiner's other epistemological works. I wanted to give these "a last chance." Strictly without looking into the more esoteric works, I wanted to understand these epistemological works by themselves alone. After about half-a-year, I knew what direction I had to take. I saw the errors I had made and the misunderstandings (felt as understandings) I had committed. I realized that the level of real understanding is not the level used in the other sciences but is, minimally, the level of living, experienced thinking, i.e., the process not the thought. From this moment on (about 1958), I slowly began on the path of inner schooling. In 1969, I met Massimo Scaligero, the Italian anthroposophical thinker. As a matter of fact, our real and effective meeting did not occur personally, but only through his books *after* personal acquaintance. Out of this, a deep and helpful friendship emerged which still lasts after his death—he died in 1980—although there was more than one question on which we did not agree. Our agreement was perfect, however, concerning questions of knowing and the inner path.

Beginning in 1965, I began to work with groups of friends and, in 1966, I began to lecture in Austria, Switzerland and Germany.

I should mention one other great and, for me, important friendship. In 1979 I made the acquaintance by mail of the eminent French anthroposophist, Mme S. Rihouet-Coroze. Our acquaintance began when, at eighty-eight years of age, she decided to translate into French my book, *Becoming Aware of the Logos*. Our friendship lasted only two-and-a-half years on earth: she died in 1982.

From the beginning my interest in Anthroposophy has been in the study of consciousness and related themes. Very soon, therefore, I was led to the idea of the *logos*. For the past twenty or twenty-two years the Prologue to St. John's Gospel has been my central meditation. Hence, all the books I have written have to do with this theme.

After the War, I had to decide to study something, but it was unclear what I should choose. I made my decision by looking towards those subjects with which, at that time, I had no relation. In this way, I chose natural science and, in particular, chemistry. I became a physical chemist and worked for thirty years in a Technical University, teaching physical chemistry—especially colloid chemistry—and doing research in the fields of adsorption, catalytic processes, surface chemistry and chemical engineering. I also have some inventions to my credit.

At the age of fifty-seven, I retired. I am now working mostly in the fields of linguistics, psychology and epistemology. These I consider to be the characteristic sciences of the consciousness soul. I am happy to have had the opportunity to have studied natural science. One can certainly learn thereby to think scientifically—and to construct a true science of the spirit such thinking must clearly be at work. Spiritual science, as sketched by

Steiner, still awaits scientists able to practice science on a higher level than the known sciences. I feel it to be my task in life to convey the fundamentals of this new science.

When I was young, I studied music — the piano — and wanted to be a musician. But this has remained only a wish. My greatest musical experience has been to hear Kathleen Ferrier sing — alas, I never heard her sing when she was alive! Among composers, excluding those of the classical and romantic periods, Bartok is most important to me. For me, he represents the music of the consciousness soul. In literature, I learned a great deal from Aldous Huxley — perhaps things he did not intend — but I have, anyway, a great inborn sympathy with him. As for poets: Hölderlin, Rilke, above all, and then Celan, with a special love for Dante, to read whom I learned Italian — which led me to Rome and to the meeting with Scaligero. About 1967, I met Zen Buddhism — a meeting which affected my life most powerfully. I think Anthroposophists could learn much from *ancient* and *Japanese* Zen. About the contemporary Zen of the White Man, however, I think differently.

Finally, let me mention two other authors who have influenced me: Tolkien and Michael Ende, whom I know personally. Of course, I have read everything that any seeker reads — philosophy, the esoteric traditions, linguistics, mythology, ethnology, history of religions, etc. — but I don't think any of it has had a special influence on me as I am today.

Anything else? This is the largest and most important question, but it is precisely the one that I cannot answer here. My consolation is that I am not alone in this. A bird singing and sitting in my window, the snow glittering in the garden, the sea on a stormy morning, the sound of a hawk, the smile beginning on a beloved face, the first caress of a hand, surely all of this and so many other "small" events had perhaps a greater bearing on my life than all that I could say. You the readers must be contented with the results. I am grateful for your interest.

GEORG KÜHLEWIND,
13 March 1984